success
handbook for
salespeople

PAUL J. MICALI

CBI PUBLISHING COMPANY, INC.
51 Sleeper Street
Boston, MA 02210

Library of Congress Cataloging in Publication Data

Micali, Paul J.
    Success handbook for salespeople.

    Includes index.
    1. Selling—Handbooks, manuals, etc.
I. Title.
HF5438.25.M536   658.8'5   81-10102
ISBN 0-8436-0853-6   AACR2

Printed in the United States of America

Printing (*last digit*): 9 8 7 6 5 4 3 2 1

contents

v

preface

The daily struggle between prospects and salespeople continues to intensify. Prospects want the best deal at the best price. But, the ability of salespeople to negotiate price on territory today is extremely limited. In many cases, it's nonexistent. The result? The modern selling function is more complex than ever, requiring more strategies and greater stamina. For salespeople, "survival of the fittest" is now a truism.

Success in sales has always been directly proportional to one's mastery of the art of convincing. But to succeed in today's fiercely competitive, computerized marketing world requires survival skills as well. These survival skills involve more than a thorough knowledge of selling techniques. While salesmanship is still the name of the game, other factors come into play on a daily basis that are just as important. One's attitude, voice, ability to communicate, creativity, assertiveness, stress threshhold, and general health are only some of them. These factors can directly influence your success or failure.

Lacking an awareness of these factors or the ability to monitor them, it is no surprise that many salespeople have been left by the wayside. Too many. But you won't be one of them. Already in your hands is the handbook that will help you survive and bring you more success than you ever thought possible. Congratulations for taking this positive step.

one

BUILD A WINNING ATTITUDE

It has often been said that man is his own worst enemy. What this means, of course, is that most of the problems we encounter in life are caused by ourselves. Oh, sure, there are always rationalizations—excuses, if you will, that place the blame on others, on economic conditions, on the environment, and even on fate. But deep down in our hearts we know, and may sometimes admit, that we need not look beyond ourselves for the real cause of our problems.

THE IMPORTANCE OF SELF-ANALYSIS

This is especially true of outside salespeople. Why? Because so much of their time is spent very much on their own. They have no supervisor who knows, on a daily basis, everything that's going on. Were they on territory on time, for instance, and did they put in a full day, say the right things, see the right people,

3

and concentrate on the right products? These and countless other questions can only be answered by the outside salesperson; all too often, however, such questions are never asked. This freedom to make decisions for themselves, while preciously guarded, may well be self-defeating for outside sales personnel. And the situation is apt never to change. How can it? How much time in each month can a sales manager spend on territory with the salesstaff? Maybe one or two days, if the district is small; and only one or two days every six to eight weeks, if the district is medium-sized to large. That is hardly enough time to "put out the fires," let alone offer corrective supervision. At all of the sales management seminars that I have conducted, I have made this statement: "The supervision of outside salespeople is at best lousy." Not one attendee has ever disagreed—because it's true.

This being the case it behooves you, as a salesperson, to take a hard, objective look at yourself. And you should do this on a regular basis, particularly when things aren't going too well. Then, and only then, can you correct situations that are self-defeating and that hamper your forward progress, if not your entire selling career.

START WITH YOUR ATTITUDE

To properly take that hard, objective look at yourself, you must begin by thoroughly examining your general attitude. How *is* your attitude towards yourself, your prospects and customers, and your company?

Let's start with yourself. Do you think you're good at what you do? It's perfectly okay to think that you are. A healthy self-image is not the same thing, however, as conceit. It is a well-known fact that people who taste the slightest amount of success in selling will almost immediately develop an ego that sometimes becomes insufferable. And an egotistical attitude can spell defeat. What should your attitude towards yourself really be? You should feel that you can do the job and will do it. You should also feel that you will do it well. At the same time, you should have a strong, intense desire to learn as much as you can in order to do the job better. Because unless you become more effective at selling as each week goes by, you will automatically put a ceiling on the amount of success that you will realize. This conclusion is based on the fact that there are only so many selling hours per day, and only five working days in a week. Accordingly, the amount of success you enjoy now will only increase in proportion to an increase in your effectiveness over the same period of time. If you're committed to steady improvement and feel determined to resist self-satisfaction and conceit, then your attitude can be considered a positive one.

Your attitude towards your prospects and customers deserves serious consideration as well. These are the people you depend on. They provide you with the orders, the cooperation, and the other essential ingredients of your success. Yet many salespeople hold improper attitudes toward their prospects and customers. By improper I mean that either they do not treat these people as well as they should, or they treat them altogether too well, to the point of subservience.

First let's talk about not treating them well enough. In this situation, the salesperson fails to respect the wishes of prospects and customers. And I don't mean wishes that are beyond the call of duty. I mean wishes such as one's preference to be called on in the morning and never in the afternoon; or another's desire to see salespeople on Tuesdays and Thursdays only; or the request of still another to be called on only when he is in his main store or main buying office. Many salespeople will balk at such wishes, maintaining that they are unreasonable. After all, they protest, why do I have to adjust my itinerary to suit them? The fact remains, however, that prospects and customers are the people who give you business. And if you are not interested in doing business with them at the times and places they request, then they will find someone else who is. That's the point to keep in mind constantly. There is hardly a salesperson left in the world who does not have a competitor.

Consequently, you can't really afford not to respect the wishes of a buyer when it is at all possible to do so.

By the same token, however, you must not swing completely to the other end of the spectrum. Avoid placing your buyers on a pedestal. Never approach buyers with the attitude that everything they say is right, that they can do no wrong, that they are to be agreed with under any circumstance, and that anything they want they must get. If you do, and if your customer is thanked profusely after every order, you will have communicated the message, "Gee, thanks. I appreciate this big favor you did for me by giving me an order." Nothing could be more damaging or wrong. There is absolutely no reason in the world why any salesperson should go to this extreme. If you have ever taken this attitude towards a buyer, you can easily straighten yourself out by realizing that customers only give you orders because the product or service you sell is useful to them. If it weren't, you wouldn't get their orders. In other words, you are doing your buyers as much of a favor by selling to them as they are for you by buying from you. Everything is even. There is no need for either party to feel indebted to the other because both gain from the transaction. That's what business is all about. Of course, this doesn't mean that you should act as though you don't really care whether you get an order or not. Under those conditions you would be forgetting that all buyers are human. And they are, make no mistake about it. They are no better than you are and should always be treated on an equal basis, but as humanly as possible, as politely as possible, and with the use of sound business ethics.

Now, how about your attitude towards your company? Believe it or not, this is a problem for many people who sell. They do not have a particularly high regard for the companies they represent and make no bones about it. They will even discuss their complaints with buyers and then wonder why strained relationships with company officials develop later on. If you do not have high regard for your company and do nothing but run it down, there is only one answer: get out of that company right now. You will never succeed to any great degree if you are not happy with the conditions that exist within your company. And the time you spend complaining about them could be used much more profitably in the selling aspects of your career. There is no sense in continuing along such a blind road when you may eventually make the change anyway. So—I repeat—if you don't like the company you're with, don't talk about it. Find a company that you can be happier in. The move will be much better for you and for your present company as well.

But let's assume that everything is fine between your company and you. You get along with your superiors, you like the way the company does things, you like the products, and you approve of the way they're marketed. Under such circumstances, why should you examine your attitude towards your company? Because there are times, even though everything is fine, when salespeople are tempted to sell the company down the river in an effort to get big orders from their buyers. For example, a customer may surprise you one day with an offer to buy a carload of your product if the price is right. What is the right price? Usually it's a price determined by the customer in advance. Now you're expected to phone your company's headquarters and okay the transaction. And many salespeople will become so excited by the prospect of such a large order that they'll grab the nearest telephone, call their home office, and expect an immediate okay. Chances are the company official will answer "no" because the price is so low that it yields no profit; still, some salespeople will insist, arguing that they must get this price because it's an important buyer, a big order, and so on. Inevitably these salespeople lose the argument and are faced with the distasteful task of relating this message to the buyer. In doing so, they run down the company. For the next several months, they will repeat this story to anyone who will listen, putting down the company each time.

This example reflects a poor attitude towards the company. Not all requests can be granted. Those that are completely unreasonable must be turned down. A good salesperson will accept this and never let such situations interfere with the company loyalty that is so important in good selling relationships. It shouldn't be hard for anyone to realize that a company pays salaries, commissions, expenses, car allowances, and more, from the profits realized in the course of doing business. When a salesperson asks the company to take a loss in order to keep a buyer happy, a lack of good judgment is being displayed. Instead of badmouthing the company to anyone—including buyers—who will listen, the salesperson should be wondering how this incident will look on the personnel records, when the time comes to be considered for promotion.

This example brings up a very important question: To whom are you, the salesperson, really responsible? When you think about it, you are really responsible to many people, including yourself. To yourself, you are responsible for doing a good job, making progress, building a career, and properly supporting yourself; you may also be responsible to your loved ones for supporting them as well. At the same time, you are responsible to the company for which you work and to the buyers who give you orders. All of these responsibilities are fairly equal in stature. It is when the balance between them is disturbed that problems occur. To feel a deeper responsibility for your buyers at the expense of your company and even yourself indicates an attitude problem that can easily be corrected when sound reasoning is applied.

POSITIVE MENTAL ATTITUDE

In the process of self-analysis, it is extremely important to determine if you have and maintain a positive mental attitude. Known as PMA, most people are well-aware of it but give it no more than lip service. At every sales meeting someone mentions the need to maintain a positive mental attitude. Everyone else agrees. No one is ever going to think negatively again. The meeting closes on an upbeat. And everyone leaves feeling stimulated and enthused. But what happens? The very next day someone remarks, "There's no point in calling on that guy again, he won't ever buy our product." Someone else insists, "There's no way that I can make my quota this month." And another person comments, "After about the 15th of December buyers just won't see you until after the new year." On and on it goes, one negative thought after another. There is nothing more devastating in sales work than a negative attitude.

Why is it that such a large segment of the population, salespeople included, routinely entertains negative thoughts? For one thing the media—newspapers, television, and radio—transmits negative news to all of us daily. As one comedian put it, "If no one broke the ten commandments there wouldn't be any eleven o'clock news." Good news may not be as dramatic as a tragedy, a murder, or a robbery. But after a steady diet of bad news, unrelieved by an uplifting event or deed, we come to see the world in very negative terms.

Upbringing, too, exerts an influence on attitude. And if you really get down to brass tacks, most of us were brought up in a negative atmosphere. As children, we repeatedly heard negative remarks from our parents. See if some of the following don't ring a bell:

"Put your boots on or you'll catch pneumonia."
"Don't get your feet wet or you'll get a sore throat."
"Do your homework or you'll fail."
"Go to bed or I'll kill you."

Each one of these statements could have been uttered in a positive manner. For example, someone could have told you: "Wear your boots so you'll stay healthy for the party Friday night." But negative messages—warnings, admonishments, and threats—were used instead because of the impact they carried in that form. The result? Most of us grew up wondering what was going to go wrong next, or fearing the terrible consequences of our own actions.

After so many years of a negative-type upbringing, it's very hard to become a positive thinker just because one becomes involved in sales work. What makes it even harder is the prevalence of negative influences and patterns around us that infiltrate our general attitude. To this very day, the tendency towards negativism persists. When we watch sports on television, for example, most of the commentary revolves around the people or team in the lead. The forward progress is commented on. Everything seems positive. But let the contest end up in a tie and now we must go to what is known as "sudden death." What does that mean? It means that all of a sudden our attention is directed to the loser rather than the winner. Why couldn't it be "sudden victory" and focus on the positive side?

Admittedly, it is not easy to develop a positive mental attitude and maintain it constantly. Even those who insist that they are positive thinkers will, from time to time, entertain negative thoughts. This is most likely to happen when we're confronted with a problem. Everyone has problems. But what do most people do about them? They worry. They lose sleep and become quite tense through the worrying process. You will agree, however, that worrying never solves a problem. It can be said that worrying is nothing more than negative thinking. It has no real value. When you are a bona fide positive thinker and you have a problem, this is what you do. You take a sheet of paper and write, across the top of it, the actual problem. Now you can look at it and understand it clearly. Then, using the rest of the sheet, you write down all of the possible solutions that are open to you. Finally, you pick the one that hurts the least and decide to go with it. Your problem is solved. It may not be the perfect solution—but then, real solutions to real problems seldom are. What you have is the best solution possible under the circumstances, and the freedom to go on to bigger and better things. That's positive thinking.

By now it must be clear that in order to survive in sales work one must have a positive mental attitude. Conversely, a negative mental attitude leads to self-destruction by distorting your sense of reasoning and rendering you unable to exercise common sense. Perhaps the difference between positive and negative mental attitudes can best be illustrated by a story I like to tell.

A salesman, working for a big corporation, was very excited about a sales contest that had been announced. He set his sights on the grand prize, a Caribbean cruise for two, and told his wife that she'd better start packing because they would be going. He worked extremely hard and made it. At the national sales convention there was tremendous fanfare during the announcement of the prize winners, and he was awarded the grand prize. He became the hero of the entire sales force. He enjoyed the attention and praises he received throughout the meeting, and couldn't wait for the day when he and his wife would embark on their trip.

After six weeks of anticipation, the time finally came for them to depart. They went to New York City and boarded the ship. At once they realized that the company had cut a few corners; it was obvious that they were not traveling first class. How was it obvious? There was no lavatory in the stateroom. But they were positive thinkers. Nothing was going to prevent them from having a good time. They looked around and discovered a lavatory just down the passageway, not far from their stateroom. So they said to each other, "What's the problem?" Then they proceeded to the main dining room, had a marvelous dinner, and returned to the stateroom as the ship was about to sail. Soon they bedded down for the night. Around midnight, however, the pretty wife was awakened; she was deathly seasick, literally green. She could think of only one thing: the lavatory at the end of the passageway. So she jumped out of her bunk, rushed through the stateroom door and headed straight for the lav. But halfway down the passageway she bumped into a man, a negative thinker with the very same problem, who was holding his stomach. Just as she collided with him she realized, for the first time, that she didn't have a stitch of clothing on, and she shrieked. The man looked at her calmly and said, "Don't worry, lady, I won't live to tell anybody."

ATTITUDE CHECKLIST

	Always	Some-times	Never
I have good control of my ego.	☐	☐	☐
I have a strong desire to do a better selling job.	☐	☐	☐
I have a good attitude toward myself.	☐	☐	☐
I tend to place buyers on a pedestal.	☐	☐	☐
I have a good, balanced attitude toward my prospects and customers	☐	☐	☐
I will fight hard with company officials to satisfy a customer.	☐	☐	☐
When deserved, I make critical remarks about my company.	☐	☐	☐
I find myself doing a certain amount of negative thinking.	☐	☐	☐
I worry about problems, personal and otherwise.	☐	☐	☐
In an anxious situation I expect the worst.	☐	☐	☐
I set high goals for myself.	☐	☐	☐
I am able to maintain a positive mental attitude.	☐	☐	☐

Note: See Appendix section for correct answers.

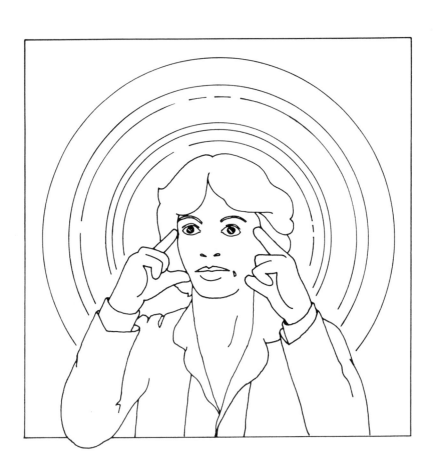

two

PERSONALITY: THE BASIC FOUNDATION OF SALESMANSHIP

All of us have heard the expression, "Before you can sell anything you must first sell yourself." But what does that really mean? It's a platitude—one of those accepted facts that no one argues with or delves into because it makes sense. Well, there's no question that it does make sense, but it's important that we do delve into it—because in its meaning lies one of the most important ingredients for successful selling.

For years I lived under the mistaken impression that most salespeople have great sales personalities; that each and every one of them had to be, and was, an extrovert. Not so. Most salespeople are *not* extroverts. First of all, let's understand the meaning of the word *extrovert*. The definition found in dictionaries is, at best, shallow. According to Webster, an extrovert is: "One whose attentions and interest are directed wholly or predominantly toward what is outside the self." When we speak of extroverts, in the selling field, we are referring to individuals who are extremely outgoing, who are aggressive yet tactful, and who consider it a pleasure to go out and meet new people. They are quick to initiate a handshake, start a conversation, and make people feel good by showing an interest in *them*. They are great to be with. And they are very much alive.

At The Lacy Institute we have been administering our sales aptitude test for years. It's a relatively simple test that measures aptitude for sales work based on an individual's responses to a series of carefully designed questions. A number of these questions are designed to measure the degree of extrovertedness in the person taking the test. After compiling the results of over ten thousand tests administered to people already involved in outside selling, some for as long as ten years, we were amazed to discover how few salespeople can be classified as extroverts. And what's worse, to the question, "Do you consider yourself an extrovert?" 67% of those taking the test answered, "No."

This confirmed a suspicion I began to develop many years ago. At that time, we conducted the Jack Lacy Course in Advanced Salesmanship at one of the charming hotels in the Back Bay section of Boston. The course ran one evening per week for eight weeks. On the first night of each course, salespeople would arrive at the hotel, seek out the function room we were using, then proceed to make their entrance. Talk about making an entrance. It was unbelievable. First they would peek inside, as if to make sure that a ferocious lion wasn't waiting to attack them. Then, looking somewhat relieved, they would enter the room on tiptoe heading directly to the last row of chairs. Not until that last row was filled would anyone consider occupying a seat in the second-to-last row. On rare occasions, a few outgoing people would walk down the length of the center aisle and take a seat in the second row from the front—but never in the first. In fact, once we realized this, we would place the first row of chairs rather close to the platform. Then, just before starting the meeting, we would instruct the hotel porters to remove the front row chairs and place them in the rear, so that those who had braved the second row would now occupy the first. We literally had to play games.

Now these people were already in sales. They were making sales calls every day. They came because they were interested in self-improvement, and they were the better salespeople. The better ones always want to improve. The poor ones stay home and watch the tube. (Our research has proved this most conclusively.) But, if the better ones behaved like introverts, what could possibly be expected of those whose selling skills were only mediocre?

PROJECTING YOUR PERSONALITY

Watching these people make their entrances reminded me of one of the most influential factors involved in sales work: the **first impression.** Regardless of where you are in your selling career, a great deal of your success depends on your personality and how you project it. A poor first impression can be costly. Our sales personalities must be such that, from the very moment of contact, the impression we create is a favorable one.

There are many who believe that good salespeople are born, not made. Nothing could be more untrue. Did you ever meet a born plumber, a born dentist, or a born lawyer? Would you board a jet plane about to be flown by a born pilot? Well, there is no such thing as a born salesperson either. Of course, some are born with a slightly greater potential for sales success than others, and some have the gift of gab while others are relatively quiet by nature. But these inherent traits do not make or break a salesperson by any stretch of the imagination. No matter what type of personality you were born with, it doesn't necessarily follow that it is sales-oriented.

Our purpose here isn't to change your personality; in fact, it can't be done. Your personality was molded, for the most part, by your parents when you were about four, five, or six years of age. They would say things like, "Don't touch that." "Put that down." "Smile at your Uncle Frank." And now that you are an adult, you *have* a personality. No one can change it for you. The only thing we can hope to accomplish is to make it more sales-oriented. And, with a little work and a lot of soul searching, this can definitely be done.

Most people don't think very much about their own personalities. Yet they are quick to pass judgment on the personalities of others. I'm certain that you have heard people make such statements as, "That guy is a jerk," and "I knew I wouldn't like her the minute I laid eyes on her ... don't ask me why, I just knew I wouldn't," or "That new man they hired has the personality of a dial tone." How easy we find it to instantly assess the personality of others. But when was the last time that you took a good, hard look at your own personality? When was the last time that you stood in front of a full-length mirror and made a presentation to the person in the glass? And did you ever ask of the person staring back at you, "Do I like how this person came across, did this person stimulate me, and would I buy from this person?"

Most salespeople neglect this kind of self-examination because they are thoroughly convinced that there is nothing wrong with their personalities. They have just enough egotism to prevent them from seeing otherwise. Yet personality is one of the biggest stumbling blocks among the nonsurvivors of the sales profession. Often these people fail to recognize the genuine cause of their difficulties, believing that the prospect, the customer, the product, or the area is to blame. What they never realize, however, is that they may have compromised the entire sales presentation right from the start, with a poor first impression.

Perhaps the best way to appreciate the role your personality plays in your work is to remember the last person who rang your front doorbell and tried to sell you something. I realize that the days of door-to-door selling are practically gone, but it still happens once in a while. Imagine that your front doorbell rings, and you wonder who might be calling on you. You open the door with expectancy. As you do, you discover a person standing there whom you've never seen before. Instantly you make a judgment. By the very appearance of this individual, you decide whether this is someone you might be interested in listening to or not. If the person is shabbily dressed and not well-groomed, you decide that you are uninterested. And you still haven't heard one word. But if the person is very presentable, you will now at least listen to the first sentence or two. Very soon thereafter you will make your final decision. You are either interested, or you are not. You take appropriate action and you take it without delay. And all of this happens in a matter of a minute or two. Frightening, isn't it? But it's so. We must face up to the fact that the personality we project makes the first impression, creates the mood, opens the door, and sets the stage—all in an extremely short period of time. It is important, therefore, that we understand personality and what it really means. Moreover, we must keep an open mind about what it takes to develop a *sales-oriented* personality.

WHAT IS PERSONALITY?

If you were asked to explain the word *personality* how would you do it? Where would you start? Personality is such an all-encompassing concept that defining it is an almost impossible task. Where sales work is concerned, perhaps the most useful definition we've been able to come up with is this: "Personality is a mental or psychic atmosphere that radiates from ourselves and produces an effect on others."

As you can see, this definition takes everything into account. The atmosphere or personality that we project is influenced by the way we look, the way we talk, the manner in which we handle people, how we shake hands, how we smile, and so forth. If the effect that we produce on others is a good one, our chances of making a sale are well above average. But if the effect we produce on others is negative, we might use any number of selling techniques and still be unable to make the sale.

Four Personality Traits That Help You Sell

Basically, there are four qualities that help make winning sales personalities. They are the qualities of being engaging, assuring, compelling, and dynamic. As we discuss each of these traits, you'll find that there is a great deal you can do to bring out these qualities in your own personality.

To be **engaging** is to make people like you, and in selling, getting people to like you is extremely important. There is no question that if people like you they will go out of their way to do business with you. In fact, some customers will pay more to do business with a person they like than with someone they don't. If, on the other hand, people do not like you, they'll avoid you like plague, allowing no possibility for you to sell them.

The question that concerns us, then, is what makes people engaging, or likeable? When I am conducting seminars I have a great deal of fun with this one. I will ask people in the audience, "Does anyone like you? Why?" Usually someone responds by describing one or two attributes that have endeared them to someone they know. Most people recommend, "Be yourself, be friendly, be generous, be sincere and warm." And when I ask, "Will that get most people to like you?" they insist that it will.

Naturally, these are all wonderful attributes but they do not represent, either individually or collectively, the real reason why most people will like you. Have you ever given this much thought? Most people have not. Yet there is only one major reason why most people will like you: because *they think that you think as they do*. People want to feel that they are on the same wave length with you. And it doesn't take much to make them feel otherwise. Consider, for example, why your next door neighbor likes you. It's probably because you mow your lawn as soon as it needs it, and because it looks nice next to his, which is also regularly mowed. But go away on vacation for two or three weeks and forget to hire someone to take care of your lawn. Then see what happens when you get back: your neighbor doesn't like you any more. You have ruined the neighborhood. Human nature is funny that way. Some of the greatest misunderstandings or hatreds develop over small things that really don't seem that important.

If you find this hard to accept, I refer you to the old saying, "Familiarity breeds contempt." What does it mean? Essentially, it means that any two people might become extremely close; but as they do, they will begin to realize the differences—sometimes very important ones—that exist between them. Their thoughts may conflict on certain issues. They may hold very different views about what's important in life. Gradually they drift apart because they just don't seem to think alike. And before long they don't see each other at all as the very familiarity that kept them together begins to breed a mutual contempt. This is why there aren't too many close friendships. If you were asked to take a sheet of paper and write down the names of twelve very close friends, could you do it? Most likely not. And it isn't because you don't want to have twelve close friends, but because you don't know twelve people who think exactly as you do. Consequently, to be close to them is very hard.

It may by impossible to form deep and lasting friendships with everyone you meet, but there are at least five ways that you can work on your personality to ensure that people will like you. By following these five simple rules, success through an engaging personality will be yours.

Never talk about yourself boastfully.   Prospects and customers are not particularly interested in hearing you tell about how great you are. This is because (and psychologists have proved it) people think about themselves 94% of the time. Therefore, when you boast about yourself, you are not talking about their favorite subject—themselves. So get in the habit of talking exclusively about others rather than yourself. If you don't think this will be appreciated, just remember the last time your brother-in-law came to your home for dinner and spent an hour telling you how great he is.

Look for the good in everyone you meet and comment on it.   You can always find something about a person to like. You may have to dig deeply in some cases, but you can find that something. When you do, make a point of commenting on it. A genuine compliment will not only endear you to that person, but will make you wonder whether you, too, possess the same good quality. Suppose, for example, that you tell someone how much you like their sport coat. Chances are you'll be rewarded with a big smile of gratitude. At the same time, subconsciously, you'll be wondering if you are equally welldressed. This keeps you on your toes.

Never volunteer opinions.   All of us know that religion and politics are sensitive subjects. For years we've been telling each other that they should be avoided, because they can lead to arguments. Well, in selling, expressing an opinion on *any* subject can get you into difficulty. After you do, you may find that you and your prospect are no longer on the same wave length. Rather than take that chance, it's a good idea to avoid volunteering opinions on any subject while selling. You should voice only your opinions on what you sell, nothing else. When your prospect expresses an opinion it is not mandatory that you also divulge yours. Better to say something like, "That's really interesting," or, "I never thought of it that way." Now, you might say, "But you're taking away my individuality, my character, my ability to say what I think." Not really. If you want to hold forth on any subject, you can certainly do so at the neighborhood cocktail party on a Saturday night when everyone else is doing likewise . There you can say whatever comes to mind. But when you're selling, you just can't afford to indulge in the pleasure of your own opinion. Most salespeople find this easy to live with except when the prospect or customer volunteers an opinion and then asks, "What do you think?" Under those circumstances, you can safely answer, "I wish I knew enough about the subject to comment on it." Your response will be truthful, because not one of us knows everything there is to know about any one subject. And, except when it comes to your own product or service, people appreciate it when you admit that you don't know as much as others. It's when you boast that they can't stand you.

Be considerate of everyone.   Keep in mind that everyone is a human being and act accordingly. Some salespeople are almost rude to receptionists and secretaries. They consider these people unimportant compared to the prospect who has the power to buy. Yet you never know who can help you along the way. If you're nice to everyone, more doors will open up for you. It's been said that kindness is something you can't give away—it always comes back to you. Here's a good test. How do you speak to your associates? In the same way that you speak to your superiors or to your garbage collector? There should be no difference whatsoever. Besides, you should like people. All people. If you don't, if you can't make yourself like anyone you meet, you are in the wrong business. In sales work, no matter what your product or service may be, you must sell it to people. You should bear in mind, on a regular basis, that all people are human, that they all have the same set of problems, they all look for kindness from everyone else, and all of them want to be treated with consideration and respect.

Smile.   It is never a good idea to be altogether too serious when selling, or at any time for that matter. A smile radiates happiness. A frown radiates gloom, and there is enough gloom throughout the world without salespeople radiating more of it. When you smile you create a good selling climate. You make people feel better for your having called on them. So remember to wear your best smile, always. I don't mean anything half-hearted or false, but a smile that comes from really liking people.

The quality of being **assuring** is what makes people believe in you. Particularly in these times of poor credibility it is extremely important that you gain the trust of others in you in order for them to do business with you. Your assurance must come across genuinely in the course of your presentation, to the degree that the prospect has enough faith in you to establish a business relationship. To develop an assuring personality, there are at least two important rules that you should follow.

Master your product or service.   Make sure that you know all that you possibly can about the proposition you are selling. Many a sales manager will tell you that if you don't know all there is to know about your product or service, don't worry about it. Consequently, some salespeople only familiarize themselves with the salient points of a product or service. Should their prospect ask questions they can't answer, they're instructed to say, "I really don't know, but I'll find out and get back to you." Well, that makes a lot of sense and it sounds most sincere. But, how many times during a sales presentation can you say to a prospect, "I really don't know," and still maintain credibility? Spend as much time as necessary to become thoroughly acquainted with what you sell. The time invested pays big dividends.

Always tell the truth.   There just isn't any place in selling for a liar. Trouble begins with the small white lie that you tell to get yourself out of a difficult situation. After a while the little white lies won't bother you, and you'll begin to tell bigger lies in order to make a sale. Soon you will be telling whoppers, and those won't bother you either. But look what happens in the process. You burden yourself with having to remember what you said to whom. Consequently, you have to store a tremendous amount of unnecessary detail in your mind, cluttering your thoughts to an impossible degree. Lying just doesn't make sense. Moreover, there is a human tendency that makes people expect the truth. You will never hear a customer say to you, "The reason I like you is because you always tell the truth." It's taken for granted that you always do—or will—until you tell just one small lie and get caught at it. From then on the expectation disappears. After that you will regularly hear, "How can I be sure you're telling the truth this time?"

The sad part is that salespeople don't realize how often they lie in order to get business. You're probably familiar with the prospect who requests, "Can we have these components in two weeks? We'll need them by then so production isn't interrupted." In this situation, some salespeople will answer, "Don't worry." They may seriously doubt that such an immediate delivery date can be met, but they don't want to lose the order. So they say, "Don't worry." This is a lie because it infers that there will be no problems with the delivery date. It is not sincere. No salesperson can survive for long in this profession without constantly telling the truth.

The third personality trait that you'll need to cultivate is the quality of being **compelling**. That's the part of your personality that gets people to act on your recommendations, and it comes into play every time you close a sale. There are two important rules to follow.

Set expectations for yourself and fulfill them.   If you are the type who keeps putting things off, missing deadlines, and constantly trying to catch up, chances are that you do not come across as a very compelling individual when selling. From now on, practice setting expectations for yourself and fulfilling them on a regular basis. This exercise will fortify your personality with a confidence that radiates so strongly when you are ready to close a sale that success will come to you more easily. Your whole vocabulary will change as you develop a source of inner strength and self-reliance. No longer will you say things like, "If you buy this product . . . ." Instead you will say, "As soon as you have bought this product, you will find. . .". When you project a compelling personality that expects nothing less than a yes, you'll find yourself getting a yes and more often than not you will get one more often. Your entire life changes once you develop this strong, compelling quality. I'm not suggesting that you overpower people. You do not apply high pressure to get what you want. The expectation I'm talking about does not exert undue pressure and is not offensive. You portray this feeling of expectancy by assuming in your own mind that you will make the sale, and you proceed according-ly. In effect, you assume the positive mental attitude that we discussed in Chapter 1. And you never let anything interfere with that type of positive thinking no matter what happens throughout the sales presentation.

Do you expect and get things from yourself regularly? Most people do not, and there is abundant evidence all around us to prove that this is so. Why is it, for example, that on April 14th of every year there are long lines of people in banks and post offices throughout the country looking for forms that are no longer available with which to file their income tax returns. They knew for one solid year that April 15th was the deadline. The government sent them the complete set of forms between Christmas and the New Year—but they lost those. Now here they are, at the last possible moment, looking for forms that are no longer available to meet a deadline that they knew about for one year. How compelling can these people be? Still another bit of proof can be found in the fact that Christmas Eve of every year is the biggest retail day in the United States. Certainly we all know that Christmas comes the 25th of De-cember each year. Around the first of December, the front page of every newspaper in the country gives a count-down of the shopping days left until Christmas. Does this get people to do their shopping before the last possible moment, before the stores are jammed and long lines have formed at every counter? Not at all. They keep putting it off until panic sets in and they rush out to buy that last present or two that should have been taken care of long before. Start today to expect and get things from yourself. You will be way ahead of the masses and you'll close more sales.

Relive your sales interviews.   Go over every sales inter-view in your mind as soon as you leave the prospect. Re-view particularly the ones that produced a sale. Don't spend too much time on the ones on which you struck out. You want to repeat your successes. By so doing, you'll develop a positive outlook which in turn promotes that quality of expectancy we've been talking about. When you make a presentation, you will expect and get an order. And when you review that presentation, you will remember how your positive expectations led to a successful sale. This process will give you the reinforcement you need to keep exercising the compelling part of your personality constantly, no matter what it is that you are doing.

The quality of being **dynamic** is by far the most difficult to achieve. Many people, blinded by egotism, believe that they already possess it. In truth, however, the number of people in this world who are *really* dynamic is practically negligible. In some rare instances, the dynamic personality is instinctive. But in the few cases per 10,000 people that it is worked for and achieved, the end result is arrived at only through diligent effort and perseverance. Developing a dynamic personality involves that much work because it requires a balanced combination of the engaging, the assuring, and the compelling qualities already discussed. It's this balance that is of the greatest importance. If you work too hard at getting people to like you, you can become overbearing. But you can't overdo truthfulness either. If you were constantly to remind your prospects, "And I'm telling you the truth... and I'm telling you the truth" they'd assume that you must be lying. In addition, you don't want to become so compelling that you get yourself thrown out. The essence of a dynamic personality lies in a balanced combination of all three qualities, plus two other virtues—**confidence** and **enthusiasm**.

Let's discuss confidence first. Where does it come from? Most people, when asked this question, will say that it comes from within. But what does that mean, "from within?" From the liver? Isn't it about time that we nailed down this business of confidence and where it really comes from? Certainly you don't believe those ads which read, "Buy my book for $4.95 and you'll have all the confidence you need for the rest of your life." While it is true that you can obtain a great deal of knowledge from a book, I rather doubt that you can gain lasting confidence from any printed page.

To determine the true source of confidence, one need only apply common sense. Haven't you noticed that whenever you do something over and over again you get progressively better at it? Haven't you also noticed that when you're doing something for the first time you have lots of reservations in your mind. Yet, when you do something that you've done many times before you don't even consider the possibility of failure. That's confidence, isn't it? And it's obvious that confidence comes from practice. That's the word: *practice*. Few things can be nailed down to one word, but confidence can.

For years we've been training salespeople to follow a very useful routine. Start practicing it yourself, before you make another sales call. On the way to a meeting with your prospect, turn off the radio in your car. Then start rehearsing. If you're on the way to see Mr. Jones, think about what Mr. Jones is like and how you're going to handle him. Then you go over your entire presentation with him, anticipating his moves. If he says this, you'll say that. If he objects to the price, you'll answer him this way. You end up by asking for the order and you get it. That's right, you are practicing. Now notice what happens when you get there. It's the second time for you and the first time for him; he's at a disadvantage. He's barely given a thought to the fact that you were coming. You will be absolutely amazed at how closely the pseudointerview in your car will parallel the real thing when you get there. If you do this routinely you'll begin to feel that you can second-guess almost anybody. Don't be led astray, however. There will be times when you will miss the boat completely. But more often than not you will come very, very close because you've gone over that road before and you have a reasonable feel for how things are going to come out.

In sales work you can never practice too much. The more of it the better. Try a new presentation on members of your family before you give it to anyone else. Try it on yourself in a full length mirror. Try it with anyone who will listen and give you comments. You just simply cannot do it enough.

There's a story that relates to our discussion; it's about a big Texan who went to New York City in his huge limousine. He maneuvered for hours through heavy traffic in search of Carnegie Hall without success. Finally, in desperation, he decided he would ask someone. He saw a little old man carrying a violin case and figured he must know. So he rolled down his window and yelled, "Pardon me, sir, but can you tell me how you get to Carnegie Hall?" The musician smiled and answered, "You practice, you practice, and you practice."

Like confidence, the quality of *enthusiasm* also requires effort. Enthusiasm comes from getting excited about what you do. If you can't get excited about what you do, then you should get another job because you will never do this one well. In fact, you probably won't survive. But if you can muster the enthusiasm necessary for sales work by constantly being excited about what you do, attaining success will not be a major task.

I'm sure you've heard many people say, "How I hate Monday mornings." What they are really saying is that they don't like their jobs and can't get excited about a new week or the new challenges it brings. Consequently, they'll always be wanting in enthusiasm. I have a friend who claims that he has a formula for getting excited about each and every day. He recommends that immediately upon awakening you should throw over the covers, leap out of bed and, with arms raised victoriously, shout, "This is a new day, and am I excited." Besides, he says, most people die in bed so you should get the hell out of there as quickly as possible.

Thirty years ago I started in sales work by joining a company called Endo Products. It is now a division of DuPont known as Endo Laboratories. I shall never forget the first sales meeting I attended. It was conducted by the president of the company, Joe Ushkow, who was such a dynamic individual that he left an impression on everyone he met. At the outset of that meeting he asked each of us to stand up and give our personal definition of salesmanship. When we were through he said, "You are all on the right track, but let me give you my own definition of salesmanship. As far as I'm concerned, salesmanship is nothing more than a transfer of enthusiasm. If you can transfer your enthusiasm about your products to the people you are trying to sell them to, more often than not they will buy." How right he was. In the years that followed, I found it to be true over and over again. If you are enthusiastic about what you sell, your chances of selling increase a hundredfold. Moreover, when you can remain constantly enthusiastic about your job, your products, and everything you do, you will be able to bounce back quickly should you lose an order you thought you were going to get. We all know that you can't sell everybody. Every so often we're bound to experience disappointment. Nevertheless, we've got to bounce back for that next call, and an enthusiastic person always finds it easier to do this, without bringing along the disappointment experienced earlier. The benefits of enthusiasm are just too numerous to mention.

Finally, one other item must be covered as it relates to personality. Many people find it difficult to control their tempers. In sales work this can be devastating. Never can you afford to lose your temper, to any degree, with anyone who represents a potential buyer. As you work on becoming an even more sales-oriented personality, make an assessment of how well you control your temper. And don't make the mistake that some people do, who control their tempers while selling but unleash any pent-up emotions when they come home at night. This is not very fair to your family. It has often been said that selling requires tremendous patience. By practicing, you can gain the patience necessary to succeed in selling—the same patience that will enable you to control your temper. The next time you feel your temper rising, stop talking. Do some listening instead. This gives you a chance to cool off. At the same time you can say to yourself, "It is immature to lose my temper and say things that I might be sorry for." People who have a temper problem cannot correct it overnight. With some intensive self-training, however, it can eventually be controlled. Those who work at it will also, indirectly, be developing the compelling personality that we discussed earlier in this chapter.

PERSONALITY CHECKLIST

	Always	Some-times	Never
I come across as an extrovert.	☐	☐	☐
I give some thought to my personality.	☐	☐	☐
Lost sales have been due to my personality.	☐	☐	☐
I tend to boast about myself.	☐	☐	☐
I look for the good in everyone and comment on it.	☐	☐	☐
Volunteering opinions is something I'm apt to do.	☐	☐	☐
While selling, I maintain a friendly smile.	☐	☐	☐
To get an order I may tell a white lie.	☐	☐	☐
I expect and get things from myself.	☐	☐	☐
I make it a point to relive each sales call.	☐	☐	☐
On the way to a sales call, I rehearse it in my mind.	☐	☐	☐
Getting started on a Monday morning is difficult.	☐	☐	☐

I look forward to each
sales call.

Generating enthusiasm
is easy for me.

Exercising patience is
something I can do.

I am able to control my
temper.

Note: See Appendix section for correct answers.

three

COMMUNICATION IS VITAL

A salesperson must never underestimate the importance of being a good communicator in order to succeed. Take any group of salespeople, all displaying equal qualities, and the most articulate communicator among them will regularly come out on top. This is because salesmanship has been justifiably called "the art of convincing." And, to convince anybody of anything, you must be skillful in the art of communicating.

THEY MUST UNDERSTAND YOU

In order to be understood it is essential that we be heard. Many who sell fail to realize this, or they forget. When you speak to someone you are doing two very significant things. With your words you are selling ideas by appealing to your listener's intellect, and with your voice you are appealing to the subjective, feeling person that every listener is. If your voice is not loud or clear enough for your listener to understand what you are saying, all efforts at communication are lost. Yet most people actually reduce their tonal volume to such a degree that it would require an extremely keen sense of hearing to discern their message.

Make Yourself Heard

You can begin to address this problem by assuming that most people have a normal sense of hearing. Rarely will you find someone whose hearing is much above normal. By speaking too quietly, you force your listener to concentrate much more than usual in order to catch every pearl of wisdom. Assuming the theory that we are all as lazy as we dare to be, your average prospect or customer will not appreciate having to do this. Furthermore, we must realize that an older person's hearing is apt to have deteriorated due to the aging process. (And many people who are hard of hearing, even in this day and age, refuse to resort to the sophisticated hearing aids currently available.) When you take all of these factors into consideration, you will have to agree that it makes a great deal of sense to project your speaking voice on a constant basis.

Not too long ago, a salesman who had taken one of our courses was having trouble closing a very large sale with a potential new account. Several times he sat down with his sales manager to develop strategy, then returned to make his presentation to the same buyer. The answer he received was always the same: "We'll think it over." He knew that this particular sale would practically double his territorial volume—that's how important it was to him. Yet it just seemed impossible to get his foot in the door. His sales manager finally called me and asked if I would consider making a call on this account with the salesman involved. She felt that perhaps I could help him close the sale, and if not, make a determination as to whether or not this account could be sold at all. The necessary arrangements were made and we made the call together. I asked the salesman to forget how many times he had been there, to start from scratch, and to make a complete presentation. I felt that if I heard the whole story I could better determine whether the sales strategy was correct. The salesman did a marvelous job. He used all of the techniques necessary to properly sell his service. He displayed a fine sales personality, used visuals, smiled at the right places, and did just about everything that you could ask of someone in a professional selling situation. I did notice one thing, however, and it involved his ability to project. In the beginning of the interview, fired with enthusiasm, he came through very clearly and with plenty of tonal quality. But as the presentation progressed, his volume decreased. Towards the end he was not only speaking less enthusiastically, but his volume was also down considerably from the time he had started. When he asked for the order he was given the usual answer: "It sounds very good. We'll think about it and let you know."

When we returned to the car we reviewed the entire interview, trying to determine what went wrong. It was quite obvious that his selling attempt was professional, and my only comment to the salesman was that he seemed to lack enthusiasm towards the end of the interview. He agreed but felt that by then we had gotten down to the unimportant details of the cost of the service and its many variations in connection with the monthly billing that would be involved.

The next day I called the buyer myself. I explained to him the real reason why I had accompanied this salesman, and asked for his help in determining the reason why this person, who seemed very successful in other aspects of his work, could not succeed in selling him. The elderly, most refined buyer was delighted to hear from me. We chatted about the young salespeople of today and how most of them are less equipped to do the job than they might be. After a very warm and lengthy conversation he finally came to the point. He said, "You know, I like that boy and I really would like to give him the business.

As a matter of fact, I am not completely satisfied with the company that's handling our accounts receivable now. To make a switch would be a refreshing change, provided that the costs were more reasonable and the service better than what we are getting. And speaking of cost," said the buyer, "it seems that every time this young fellow comes in and tells me what a good job he can do for me, he begins to mumble when we get down to just how much it's going to cost. I don't understand everything he's saying. I'm embarrassed to admit that I don't wear a hearing aid and that's why I keep telling him that I'll think about it. Really, I'd love to know what his price structure is."

I called the salesman and explained the situation to him. I suggested that he write an immediate letter, stating that he was following up on his call and attaching a complete schedule of the services he could render, along with the costs that such services entailed. By *return mail* he received a letter stating that the buyer was ready to give him his business and would he please come in and make the necessary arrangements.

Make Yourself Clear

Once we have learned to open our mouths and speak loudly enough, the next thing to consider is clarity. Speaking clearly is not at all difficult. It is simply a case of being completely aware of each word we speak.

Let us suppose that you received a typewritten letter. Let's further suppose that the letter contained no capital letters, no periods, and no paragraphs. What you received was a page of several hundred words all run together. Imagine how hard it would be to read this letter and properly digest its contents. Well, that's how many people talk. They simply go on and on, often in a monotone, without ever breaking off a sentence to separate it from the next. Remember, then, that sentences end

with a period and that there is a space between the end of one
sentence and the beginning of the next, exactly as in the properly typewritten letter.

Running words together is an even greater problem. Clarity is sacrificed to a tremendous degree when this is done. For
example, you'll often hear people say "didja" for "did you,"
"whenya" for "when you," and "seeya" for "see you." If we
know the person who is speaking, we are usually able to understand what is being said. But when listening to someone we
have just met, whose method of speaking is unfamiliar to us,
their tendency to run words together can be a disastrous im-
pediment to good communication.

When you run together words that are poorly enunciated,
you force prospects to be unusually alert in order to figure out
what you are trying to tell them. They must listen for your key
word, then go back and decipher the entire sentence. In doing
so, they miss part of your following sentence. Soon the entire
thrust of your presentation is lost. By not speaking clearly you
are actually expecting your listeners to perform mental gym-
nastics. More often than not, you are expecting far too much.
That's right. You are expecting a sustained effort on their part
to decipher what you are saying and figure out what it all
means.

Let's talk about sustained effort. Did you ever stop to consider how difficult it is to sustain the effort of doing anything?
Let's conduct an experiment that will drive the point home
very clearly for you. Hold out your left arm at shoulder height,
with index finger pointing straight ahead. Pointing straight
ahead and with your left arm completely extended, you're going to hold this position for two minutes. Time yourself with
your watch. Be sure to keep your arm completely straight. At
the end of this time period you will find that your arm has
become extremely heavy, and maybe even somewhat painful.
In fact, during the second minute you'll actually find it an effort to hold this position. Your arm is one of the most powerful
parts of your body, yet only with difficulty does it stand up
under two minutes of sustained effort. Imagine, then, the

mental effort you impose upon your prospects, who must struggle for much longer periods in an attempt to interpret the sounds you are making. Is it any wonder that they lose interest in what you are saying?

Careless enunciation can easily rob you of your effectiveness when putting yourself across verbally. This habit may be hurting your performance, and yet you may be totally unaware of its existence. People never tell you that you speak indistinctly. They simply turn you off.

To improve your enunciation is not difficult and, by the way, has nothing to do with the speed with which you talk. It is impossible to talk faster than people can understand—if you enunciate clearly. You have probably marveled at the rapidity with which sports announcers can speak and yet be so well understood. A blow by blow description of a prizefight is a perfect example. Each punch is described as quickly as it's thrown—and many times they come fast and furiously. The secret is good enunciation. Sports commentators are not only aware of its importance, but they work at it. They listen to tapes of themselves to make sure that every word of their rapid-fire delivery comes through crisp and clear.

Exercises in Enunciation

Precise enunciation begins with an understanding of how the act of speaking is physically accomplished. Air that comes up from your lungs strikes your vocal cords, producing sound. Then, using chiefly your tongue, lips, and jaws, you convert that sound into words. The process of that conversion determines how much clarity there is in your enunciation.

Relax the lips.   The sounds of *p* as in Paul and *b* as in boy are formed with the lips. If you utter them with relaxed instead of tense lips, you will become easier to understand. You can demonstrate this fact to yourself right now by saying aloud: "Brendon Bracken brought Beaver Brooks' brother Benjamin." It is virtually impossible to speak this phrase unless your lips are completely relaxed. How do you relax your lips? Try imitating the sound of a motorboat by blowing air between them and allowing them to flop loosely up and down. Do this several times. Now try to achieve the same effect with your lips, this time without making a sound. Then repeat the statement three times without stopping: "Brendon Bracken brought Beaver Brooks' brother Benjamin." If on the second and third time you sounded better than the first, it's because you were able to relax your lips. Consequently, the sound of *b* was easier for you to make, enabling you to enunciate in such a way that people could easily understand it.

Relax the tongue.   The sounds of *t* and *d* are formed chiefly with the tongue. Say the following sentence aloud: "I think that I ought to tell Tom the time." Now relax the tongue. You can do this by imitating a machine gun—by blowing your breath out and letting your tongue flop up and down against the roof of your mouth as you do so. At first this may be difficult, but after a few tries you'll find that it's rather easy. After you have practiced the machine gun exercise a few times, try the statement again: "I think that I ought to tell Tom the time." If you found this statement easier to pronounce clearly, it means that you have improved your enunciation by relaxing your tongue.

Relax the jaws.   Now let's tackle the sounds of *g* and *j*. These sounds are formed chiefly with the jaws. First of all, say the following statement aloud: "Jimmy and Johnny were juggling jugs of juice." This won't be easy to say unless your jaws are completely relaxed. Here is a simple exercise for the jaws. With the lower jaw hanging as loosely as possible, shake your head as if you were shaking water from your face and hair. Let the jaw flop back and forth as loosely as you can. After you have done this a few times, take a deep breath and repeat the statement three times: "Jimmy and Johnny were juggling jugs of juice." As you say it you will find that it becomes increasingly easier to enunciate the many *j*'s in the sentence as your jaws become completely relaxed.

I am not by any means suggesting that you must engage in these exercises every day to enunciate clearly. More important is that you understand how to relax the lips, the tongue, and the jaws, and that you use this awareness to improve your habits of enunciation. But if you are about to make a sales presentation or address a large group and find yourself unusually tense, doing these exercises in advance will prove extremely helpful.

Form mental images.   Another way to ensure proper enunciation is to formulate mental images of the exact spelling of the words being used. For instance, a majority of Americans will say "noozpaper" instead of "newspaper." Yet they say "few" instead of "foo." The correct enunciation of *new* is rarely heard. Surveys have shown that the most commonly used words are the ones that are most likely to be poorly or incorrectly pronounced. Many people, for example, say "Mundee," "Toozdee," "Frydee," "dolla," "paypa," and so on. By forming a mental image of the spelling of these words, you will find it easier to catch your mistakes in pronunciation, and can endeavor to correct them. If what you sell involves specific trade names, make sure that they are always enunciated clearly.

It is important to note, however, that the practice of good enunciation can be grossly overdone. Overly meticulous or exaggerated enunciation can be as irritating to your listener as plain sloppiness of speech. Furthermore, your clipped words will suggest a very affected individual—someone thoroughly impressed with the sound of his own voice and the manner in which he speaks. The main point to remember is that clear enunciation is imperative for verbal communication but it must not be exaggerated to the degree that it becomes obvious—or even annoying.

Read aloud.   One of the best ways to improve your enunciation is by reading aloud whenever possible. It's a marvelous exercise because it slows down the tempo of your speech and forces you to mouth each word exactly as you see it in print. Years ago I had the pleasure of working with a well-known newscaster on radio. Naturally, before he went on the air, he would go over the yellow sheets that he had torn off the tele-type machine. But he didn't just glance over the news before reading these sheets on the air. He actually went into an un-used studio, closed the door, and read each news item aloud. This gave him a feel for the words. Not one word would be foreign to him when he went on the air. When two words in succession were rather difficult to pronounce, he would make a mark between them. That mark reminded him to pause slightly between words to avoid poor enunciation.

This dry run was something for which he always made time. His ability to speak so well and yet not draw attention to his enunciation intrigued me. I asked him about it one day. I said, "Dan, how do you constantly keep yourself from falling into the bad speech habits that we so regularly find in most people?" His answer was a very simple one.

He said, "That's easy. I read aloud at every opportunity that I have—even at home, when I'm reading a book. If you read aloud, you hear yourself speaking and you can concen-trate on how you sound as well as what you read. If you listen to yourself without watching someone's reaction, you are able to improve your speech on a regular basis."

All of us can benefit from Dan's example. When you read sales bulletins about your products or services, do you read them aloud? Better still, when was the last time you made your sales presentation to yourself—aloud?

YOUR VOICE CAN BE A GOLD MINE

We all know that success in selling can only be achieved if we get prospects to listen to our presentation. And we've just seen how important speaking clearly and enunciating well can be. But neither strong projection nor clear enunciation are enough if your prospects decide not to listen because of the *sound of your voice*. At all times your voice must be pleasing to the ear of your prospect. If it is irritating in any way the prospect stops listening and you have lost your chance to make a sale. But when it's pleasing, it can be a gold mine.

This is not a theory. It's a fact. Here's an example. When you are listening to a speaker who needs to clear his throat but doesn't, what do you do? Don't you automatically clear yours? It happens unconsciously. That's how irritating it is to your ear. It makes you respond—automatically.

Well, what makes a voice pleasing to the ear? Research has shown that the lower the voice, the more pleasing it is to the ear. Conversely, the higher the voice the more irritating it is to the listener. That's why we marvel so often at the voices of radio and television announcers. We remark on how mellow and resonant their voices are. Actually, you will find that the great majority of these professionals speak in very low-pitched voices, and it's this quality that pleases your ear.

Did you ever notice what happens to your voice when you are under stress or nervous tension? When you're trying very hard to make a sale? When you know that you're not getting through to the prospect and you're getting worried? The vocal chords tighten up and your voice becomes higher. How can you correct this? It's not hard. First, however, you'll need to understand exactly what's happening inside of you.

One of the chief reasons for the tension we experience is related to our nervous systems. We have two of them—the **voluntary** and the **involuntary** nervous systems. You can control your voluntary system and the many muscles it governs at will—your fingers, hands, legs, and other parts of your body, for example. But your involuntary system cannot be controlled at will. Your senses—like hearing and smelling— are in that system, and so are certain muscles. Normally the voluntary and involuntary systems are in balance. Neither dominates the other. Under emotional stress, however, the involuntary system will dominate, causing a number of problems. One of these is the tightening of your vocal chords, raising the pitch of your voice. Other problems include butterflies in the stomach, sweaty hands, and trembling knees.

Surprisingly enough, however, you *can* relax your involuntary nervous system. This is because the relaxing of any muscle in your body also causes the relaxation of the nerve connected to that muscle. And this nerve, in turn, relaxes certain cells in your brain that are connected to it.

A Short Course in Diaphragmatic Breathing

The diaphragm is the largest muscle in your body and is controlled by the involuntary nervous system. By relaxing the diaphragm you can exercise a relaxing influence throughout the entire involuntary nervous system. Because it is controlled by the involuntary nervous system, however, you cannot directly relax your diaphragm at will. But, since the diaphragm is located at the floor of your lungs, you *can* relax it indirectly through specific breath control exercises. Technically, this is known as **diaphragmatic breathing.** In the next few minutes you are going to learn how to wipe out tension and greatly improve your voice. And since this also allows more oxygen to enter your blood stream, you will feel better and have much more energy. That's right. You're going to learn a diaphragmatic breathing technique that will pay you huge dividends for the rest of your life.

Remember your school gym teacher who would bellow: "OK, it's time for some deep breathing exercises. Inhale— chest out, stomach in—exhale. Again: chest out, stomach in, inhale, exhale." Actually, this was a great way to expand the chest, inflate the lungs to maximum capacity, and take in additional oxygen. However, it did absolutely nothing in the way of relieving tension. In fact, it increased it.

You can prove this to yourself right now. Place your left hand on your chest and your right hand on your waist. Now inhale. Observe how much your chest actually rises and to what degree your stomach is pulled in. Now exhale. Note that the chest goes down to normal position and the stomach comes out. Now inhale once more, this time holding your breath for as long as you possibly can. Note the tenseness in the small of your back. If the breath is held long enough, this tension turns into actual pain. This is due to muscular tension which, in turn, creates nervous tension. This type of deep breathing is actually creating more tension in your diaphragm, instead of relaxing it.

Diaphragmatic breathing has the opposite effect. It relaxes the diaphragm, puts more oxygen in your blood stream, and makes your voice more resonant. Here is how you take a diaphragmatic breath. As you inhale, make a special effort to leave the chest where it is. Do not raise it or attempt to push it out. Place your left hand on it and make sure it stays in place. Then place your right hand on your stomach. Now, as you inhale air, push your stomach out. If your hand moves forward, you'll know that you are pushing it out. Do this a few times to get used to the method. Take in as much air as you can. You may experience a little dizziness. If so, stop for a minute and then resume. The dizziness is nothing to worry about. It is caused by fresh oxygen penetrating the lower cells of your lungs. They have been dormant so long that they house stagnant air. As you clean them out and substitute wholesome, oxygen-filled air, you are apt to get somewhat dizzy.

Repeat this diaphragmatic breathing exercise several times until you are able to hold your chest motionless while pushing the stomach out. You can easily check to make sure that you are doing this correctly, by expelling all of the air in your lungs and placing your hands on your stomach, just above the waist. Make sure that the tips of your middle fingers are touching. Now inhale deeply, pushing the stomach out as you do. If the tips of your fingers become separated (about one to two inches apart) you are doing the exercise correctly. Practice this at least twelve times in a row.

You have now mastered the technique known as diaphragmatic breathing, and you have also learned how to relax yourself at will. Your physical power will now increase, your general health will improve, and whenever you are under pressure, you will know how to get immediate and substantial relief from tension. You will be able to remain calm, think clearly, and handle a situation to your own satisfaction. When you speak while under pressure, your voice will contain no trace of tension. This will do wonders for your confidence, along with your ability to put yourself across.

If you want to prove to yourself that diaphragmatic breathing offers you complete relaxation, here's a simple test. Spread your hands and fingers lightly across your stomach and laugh heartily. Feel your diaphragm vibrating? That's why people want to laugh, whether they realize it or not. Vibrations have a relaxing effect on the diaphragm which, in turn, produces complete relaxation. And that's also why every year most of the award-winning television shows are comedies.

Do not assume that to enjoy the full benefits of diaphragmatic breathing you must give up your present breathing habits completely. Even if you take only a dozen diaphragmatic breaths each day, you will notice a difference. The more of them that you take, however, the greater the rewards. The trick is to remember to do this. All of us have the greatest of intentions, but memory and motivation don't always come into play at the right time. It's important, therefore, that you develop certain helpful reminders.

If you drive your automobile for a substantial portion of each day, you have a built-in reminder. Every time you stop at a red traffic light, take a diaphragmatic breath. All of us use the telephone with frequency. Every time you find yourself dialing a number, take a diaphragmatic breath. You should also do this each time you begin to speak. Since we all seem to open and close a substantial number of doors in one day, perhaps you can take a diaphragmatic breath every time you find yourself with a doorknob in hand. And there is no better way to begin the morning than by doing some diaphragmatic breathing immediately upon arising.

Rich and resonant tones, which carry authority and stature, will be regularly found in the voice once the diaphragm is used while speaking. If you take a diaphragmatic breath and then speak as you exhale, you will be amazed at the improved sound of your voice. You can demonstrate this to yourself by taking a diaphragmatic breath and saying as you exhale: "From down below." Take another breath and this time say, "This is from down below." Again, take one more breath and this time say, "This is from the diaphragm from down below." Continue from there, using sentences of your own choice. Repeat them until they flow easily and resonantly. A good way to master this procedure is to read aloud, making sure that you take a diaphragmatic breath at the beginning of each sentence.

After you've done a reasonable amount of practicing, you will detect a marked improvement in the sound of your voice. You may find it difficult to notice at first because we don't hear ourselves as others do. But you can certainly find out just how much your voice has improved with this simple exercise. Face the corner of a room where there are no doors or windows close by. If you stand with your head about twelve inches from the point where the walls meet, the sound will bounce back into your ears. Now tense your throat slightly, as you would when you are about to gargle, and say, "This is a tight throat." Now relax completely, take a diaphragmatic breath, and as the air comes out of your mouth say, "This is a rich and mellow tone." The difference will astound you.

You realize, of course, that as you master diaphragmatic breathing, you are also gaining deliberate control of your diaphragm. You are doing so indirectly, but there is no question that you are achieving this control. And there's one more thing you can do, unrelated to your breathing, that will greatly help in achieving control of the diaphragm. Lift your stomach as high as you can under your chest and hold it there for a few seconds. Repeat this ten times. Most likely you are now experiencing a slight soreness in your back, near the shoulder blades. This is because the muscles that support the stomach have become soft and flabby—a major reason why so many people develop a paunch. Incidentally, if you happen to be getting a little thick around the middle, this is a quick way to take several inches off your waistline. It won't reduce your weight, however. It merely reduces the extent to which the stomach protrudes by developing the necessary strength in the muscles to hold it in place.

All of this will greatly improve your voice. And there is nothing magical about it. In fact, none of it is new or unusual. There isn't a TV or radio announcer, comedian, opera star—or any other person who depends on the voice for a living—who doesn't know about and regularly uses diaphragmatic breathing. It's a must for them and it will be a great plus for you. The average individual, when first exposed to this method, wonders about the possibility of becoming self-conscious. Won't breathing from the chest instead of the stomach appear rather silly to the prospect? Absolutely not. The listener is always looking at your face. And as you master the procedure, it will come to you rhythmically and automatically. Nobody will ever know you're doing it—but they may wonder why you sound so resonant and so convincing.

One thing is certain: without realizing it, you will begin to project better. This doesn't mean shouting. It means that, because of the lowered pitch and greater resonance of your voice, you will be easier to understand. You'll come across more clearly and exude confidence and authority while you speak. You will do a better job of convincing.

COMMUNICATION AND VOCABULARY

The tendency to use big, rarely used words can be traced to a variety of impulses. Usually it is not sparked when children are learning the English language in the classroom. Simplicity of language is the theme there. Grammar is in the spotlight.

But in rare instances, because even teachers are human, the classroom may have been the site where this impulse was originally encouraged. To this day I can recall when my seventh grade teacher was scolding a boy in my class. He had passed in a well-written assignment that contained an abundance of misspelled words. The teacher was disgusted. With an angry voice she said, "If your rewrite has one single spelling mistake, you'll cause me to excoriate with a few bitter invectives." The boy burst out laughing along with the entire class. Who understood what that meant? And now the teacher was boiling. She went to the blackboard, wrote out the words *excoriate* and *invectives*, and assigned us to write ten sentences containing these words for our homework. This forced us to look them up. Well, the next day every member of our class went out of the way to use these words in regular conversation. Using these words made us feel grown-up. Fortunately, the game died out in a few days. But some people persist in using big words where simple ones would do well into adult life, believing that these words reflect their sophistication. More often than not, however, such people appear affected and only succeed in alienating their listeners, rather than in impressing them.

Other people develop this tendency by reading articles or columns in magazines and newspapers that offer vocabulary training. They usually carry titles like "Increase Your Word Power," or "Improve Your Vocabulary," or "Know Your Language." If you examine the contents of these educational gems, you'll find the most far out, least-used words imaginable. Each new article must be even more difficult to write than the last, because their authors seem to be scraping the bottom of the barrel. The most recent one I read contained the word *parsimony*. Don't bother to look it up.

This is not to say that a thorough knowledge of the English language is unnecessary. Neither is there any harm in being interested in, and learning, the unusual and rarely used words in our language. Just don't adopt them for everyday use in selling. More often than not, prospects won't ask you what you mean for fear that they are showing their ignorance. In-

stead, they will let you go on and on without really understanding what you're saying. And when they don't understand,
they don't buy.

Make it a hard, fast rule for yourself to avoid words not
common to most people. Everyday, simple language is best for
communicating and for selling. Far too many salespeople will
make constant use of the thirty-five-cent words, claiming that
they're impressive. Impressive to whom? Certainly not to the
prospect. There is always a built-in danger that you may be
speaking over your prospect's head. Why do it? To communicate means to transmit knowledge. To do this you must be understood. Using plain, simple language is the best way to
guarantee that you will be.

Descriptive Adjectives Can Help

Speaking in plain, simple language doesn't mean that your
sales presentation must be dull. It can be made very interesting by the regular and clever insertion of descriptive adjectives
wherever possible. We all know the importance of painting
word-pictures when we are selling. But most of us don't use
this valuable, convincing tool to fullest advantage. One reason
for this is that we are usually speaking "off the cuff," letting
the words flow as they come. Consequently, our concentration
is focused on expressing the thought as crisply as possible—
which is fine. But if we wrote out a sales presentation in its
entirety, took a good look at it, and then inserted some well-
thought-out, descriptive adjectives, we would have added to
its impact considerably. Once you've supplied the adjectives in
writing, a few readings of your presentation will help you remember to use them when selling.

There's no doubt that word-pictures are stimulating. Here
are a few examples: surgically clean; pearly white; lightning-
fast; deathly afraid; screeching wheels; skyrocketing profits.
I'm sure that you get the idea. It could be called picturesque

speech. The fact remains that if you stimulate a prospect in this way—while communicating effectively at the same time— you greatly increase the amount of interest paid to what you are saying. And that's a big plus in any selling situation.

POOR SPEECH HABITS

Here, on the other hand, is a big minus for very serious consideration. It is quite possible to develop a pleasing voice, to use down-to-earth, picturesque vocabulary, and still annoy a prospect by the way you talk. The annoyance comes in response to poor speech habits that certain salespeople develop unknowingly. As with all other habits, control is lost and the remedy not even considered.

Think about the last time that you were totally irritated by someone whose speech was forever interrupted by 'ers' and 'ahs', along with the pauses to accommodate them. You felt like saying, "Will you please come out with what you're trying to say?" But you couldn't be that rude. You suffered through it. And your irritating friend wasn't even aware of the problem. It's a habit—a very bad one.

The following is a transcript from a tape recording of a radio talk show. The talkmaster was soliciting public opinion on pending gun control legislation when a man called in and made this statement (please read aloud for maximum impact):

Hi, ah, how are you? Ah . . . I'd like to, ah, add my, ah, two cents to this . . . ah . . . gun-control law, ah, you've been talking about. Ah . . . it seems to me . . . ah . . . that, ah, any adult, ah, who is . . . ah . . . say, ah, . . . twenty-one or over . . . ah . . . should be able to, ah, get a permit and, ah, own a gun . . . ah, small or large. Ah . . . after all, ah, do you realize that . . . ah . . . more people are, ah, killed each year by automobiles, ah, than by . . . ah . . . guns? To me, ah, it's absolutely, ah, crazy to . . . ah . . . limit the gun permits . . . ah, to people, ah, who have a . . . ah . . . valid reason only . . . ah . . . and deny all others. Ah, you certainly don't, ah, have to have . . . ah, a valid reason for, ah, owning

or . . . ah . . . driving a car. Yet . . . ah . . . a seventeen-year-old . . . ah . . . can get behind the, ah, wheel of a car and, ah, kill a few people . . . ah . . . the very first day.
Ah . . . ah . . . these lawmakers just don't, ah, use their heads. I say, ah, let's look at the, ah, statistics first and, ah, then arrive at conclusions about, ah . . . a gun-control . . . ah, law. Suppose . . .

At this point the talkmaster couldn't stand it any longer. The agony was too much for him, and most likely for the radio audience, too. So he politely dismissed the caller by saying, "Well, sir, you've made your point and we must move along. Thank you for calling." He couldn't possibly let this man struggle through another sentence on the air.

Let's examine what happened here. The caller had used 204 words to make his point. Of these, forty-nine were 'ahs.' Almost every fourth word was an 'ah' with a pause before and after it. To listen to him was painful. If only someone would sit him down and make him listen to himself on tape, he might realize that this horrible speech habit is hampering him every time he opens his mouth.

How do *you* sound on tape? Have you ever taken the trouble to find out? If you haven't, and many individuals have not, I suggest you place this assignment very high on your things-to-do list. You probably already own a tape recorder, but you may never have thought about this possible use for it. If that's the case, here is a good way to get a natural recording of how you really speak. With adhesive or cellophane tape, attach the recorder microphone as closely as possible to the mouthpiece of your telephone. Then phone a friend of yours and, as soon as he or she answers, press the record button. Don't tell the other party that you are recording your portion of the conversation. Keep the call as natural as possible. Once you get involved in the conversation you'll soon forget that you are recording yourself and will speak in your own natural fashion. When you play back the tape, be very critical of yourself. Forget your ego. Place yourself in the shoes of a listener and determine if the voice is pleasing to the ear, if there is enough inflection, and if there are any bad speech habits that need to be corrected.

If you don't own a tape recorder, buy one. Many cassette types sell for under thirty dollars. It will be one of the best investments you ever made. Once you develop the technique of taping yourself, be sure to go through this exercise every so often. Our speaking habits are so subject to change that one can never rest assured that all is well. It's easy to pick up words and phrases from others—some good, some bad—without even realizing it. Accents and drawls are catchy. Mispronounced words are sometimes adopted unknowingly. The perils are many.

We must all become keenly aware of our susceptibility to bad speaking habits. Some of these habits are more contagious than many of the dread diseases. They creep into our speech almost instantly and then linger indefinitely or until detected (usually by others). The insult and bore the listener, and the damage that is done can be devastating. One particularly catching example is the abrasive expression, "ya know." The growth of the 'ya know' users has been phenomenal. Everywhere you go you are apt to encounter someone in the 'ya know' rut. And the expression has lost its original meaning completely. While being told something entirely unknown to you, the "ya knows" are inserted after every third or fourth word. Ridiculous, in more ways than one.

During a recent sales seminar one of the salespeople in attendance requested permission to relate one of his experiences. He told a marvelous marketing story with a sad ending. The product didn't sell. When he was through I complimented him for remembering all the details and thanked him for sharing this knowledge with all who were present. Then I said, "Would you believe, Bill, that I counted over forty 'ya knows' while you were speaking? Have you ever tried to get rid of this habit?" His answer was a classic. "Ya know," he said, "I'm very aware that I've picked up this, ya know, habit, but, ya know, one of these days I'll get rid of it. Ya know, I used to be what you call, ya know, a chain smoker. Well, ya know, when I made up my mind, ya know, I stopped. And soon, ya know, I'm going to stop, ya know, saying, ya know." The group roared with laughter, and Bill joined them. It was funny for the moment. But consider this: a salesperson with the 'ya know' habit is much like the cab driver with worn-out shock absorbers in his aging cab. They get you there, but the ride is annoyingly bumpy.

COMMUNICATION CHECKLIST

	Always	Some-times	Never
I speak loudly enough to make certain that people hear what I'm saying.	☐	☐	☐
I tend to speak louder when communicating with an older person whose hearing may be poor.	☐	☐	☐
I make a special effort to speak clearly by not running my words together.	☐	☐	☐
I am aware of and try to improve upon my enunciation.	☐	☐	☐
I form mental images of the exact spelling of words to insure good enunciation.	☐	☐	☐
I avoid exaggerated enunciation bordering on the staccato.	☐	☐	☐
I read aloud for practice in enunciation.	☐	☐	☐
I practice and use diaphragmatic breathing.	☐	☐	☐
In selling, as well as in social conversation, I avoid uncommon words.	☐	☐	☐

My presentation produc-
es impact because I
paint word-pictures
with descriptive adjec-
tives.

I am aware of my bad
speech habit(s) and
work at breaking it
(them).

I sometimes record my
phone conversations and
play them back to de-
tect poor speech habits.

Note: See Appendix section for correct answers.

four

STAND OUT WITH CREATIVITY

A creative sale is the kind brought about by salespeople who are able to sell products and services to individuals who didn't realize they needed them. Often such salespeople come on the scene unexpectedly and in no time develop needs in the minds of prospects that lead to creative sales. This is what really keeps our economy moving.

If you look into the definition of "create" you'll find that it means: "to cause to come into existence; to produce out of nothing; to originate." I like the phrase, "to produce out of nothing." This is exactly what salespeople do when they call on prospects and create sales.

To be a creative salesperson requires a great deal of thinking—deep thinking. If this were easy, everyone would be using creative salesmanship and everyone would be extremely successful in selling. We know that this is not so. Creativity in selling may take many forms, but in every case it is the product of a good selling imagination. Your company cannot always supply the imaginative tools necessary to creative

59

selling. It is up to you, when you're face-to-face with your prospect, to exercise the creativity that will put you and your product or service over.

CREATIVITY AND LEADERSHIP

We all know that most people are followers rather than leaders. But if you are in sales you are, almost automatically, a leader. This is because every time you make a sale you have succeeded in getting someone to act upon your recommendation. You lead someone else into taking an action.

Isn't it amazing, though, that most people don't realize how much creativity this takes? They dismiss the whole idea by claiming that creativity belongs on New York's Madison Avenue, where the major advertising agencies come up with striking and original ads almost daily. They will argue that selling is one thing and advertising another—so why confuse the issue?

For salespeople to treat the subject of creativity so lightly is a great mistake. All of us are influenced by creativity on a daily basis. Think of how many times you jump into your car to make a sales call, turn on the radio, and hear a cleverly composed advertising jingle plugging a particular product. Maybe the jingle is backed by a catchy tune that tickles your imagination. If so, you may find yourself whistling or humming that tune for the rest of the day. Almost unconsciously you have learned something new that keeps coming to mind over and over again. What has really happened here? A clever songwriter has creatively composed a tune that millions of people will remember. The same situation occurs when you read a book. You learn from or you're entertained by the product of someone's imagination. The author creatively put together the words that tell the story, and millions of interested people reap the benefits. Similarly, when you visit an art museum, you spend hours admiring the many pieces of art. You comment on the colors, the subject matter, or the mood; yet it's actually the creativity of the artists that enables them to stimulate and move you. You are in awe of their talent. Inwardly you wish you had it.

Of course, no one is asking you to become a composer, to write a book, or to make paintings. But in the one thing that involves you on a daily basis—the act of professional selling—why shouldn't you want to become such a leader, the kind that others will be influenced by? Why shouldn't you strive to become just as creative in your own field? Why shouldn't you want to become so good at what you do that customers will marvel at your ability?

In deciding to do this, the first step to take is a relatively simple one. Every day, from now on, start your activities by asking yourself this question: "How can I do what I'm doing **differently and better?"** The last three words of this question are most important. If you don't regularly change what you're doing for the better, you will soon find yourself in a rut. And it's all too easy to get trapped there. As human beings, we are creatures of habit. We fall into the habit of doing the same things in the very same way. Most people argue, "If something works, why change it?" Well, maybe it could work even better. Isn't it worth a try?

To get into a rut is easy; to stay there, easier still. Little effort is required. Yet all of the greatest discoveries, the important inventions, the breakthroughs in all fields, have come about because someone dug deeply enough to find a better way. You can find a better way of doing your thing by forcing yourself to overcome tired habits with a fresh, creative approach.

Chances are that your company has supplied you with all the necessary tools to sell its product or service. So you go out, day after day, telling the story as best you can. The company has described for you all of the features and benefits. Hopefully you concentrate on the benefits. But it's the same thing over and over again. When was the last time that you took your presentation apart and tried to make it different and better? When was the last time that you added an intriguing and creative statement that would elicit a better reaction from your prospects and customers? This is what creativity is about. When you forge ahead with a sales story that is different and better, you increase your creativity and your selling successes as well.

Creativity and imagination go hand in hand. The more imagination you use in selling, the more creative a salesperson you have become. Most people give the word *imagination* a quick brush-off. They admit that it's important but do little more than that. Yet an active selling imagination can create opportunities where none seem to exist. Look at it this way: no two people buy a product or service for the same reason. Each individual buyer has a specific motive for making the purchase. When you match this motive with one of the benefits of your product or service, you are using selling imagination in its truest form.

USING THE HOT BUTTON

We've already mentioned that, according to research-based findings, people think about themselves 94% of the time. Therefore, when prospects consider a purchase, their main concern is, *"What's in it for me?"* And each prospect always has a dominant desire. We call this dominant desire the prospect's **Hot Button.** Once you have found the Hot Button you build your presentation around it. And as often as you can hit that button in the process of your presentation, the closer you are to making the sale.

The term *Hot Button* is one of the most important phrases you will encounter as a salesperson. We recognized its importance years ago and copyrighted it. That's what selling is all about. It is the key to the easy way to sell. The hard way is how most salespeople approach the whole selling process.

They are so adept at making a presentation that they virtually insist on giving their prospects the "whole dose." Every feature and benefit gets full play in the hope that prospects will single out one of them and say, "That's it. Stop. I'll buy it." But it just doesn't happen that way. Instead, the presentation is usually given without interruption. The prospect says nothing, the order is asked for, the idea is rejected, and the sales interview is over. The salesperson says, "Thank you for your time," and leaves. Most people sell in just that way. They later wonder why the prospect didn't buy. They review the entire sales interview in their minds, find nothing wrong with their performance, and dismiss the entire episode by arriving at this conclusion: the prospect just wasn't smart enough to realize how many advantages the product offers.

Today the Hot Button technique is more important in selling than ever before. People are constantly immersed in their own problems, some personal, others business-related. The best way to get prospects to set these problems aside and discuss how they may use your product or service is to zero in on their Hot Button and build your presentation around it—at every possible occasion. You might be wondering, "Well, suppose you can't find the prospect's real motive—how can you apply this technique?" You will be amazed at how easy it is to pinpoint the dominant desires of your prospects—all of them. Once you have gained their interest with an effective approach (the techniques for which we will discuss in Chapter 5), get them to talk. Let them enter into the conversation *very early in the interview.* Invariably they will "spill" their strongest needs and concerns. This technique takes advantage of the human tendency to think about oneself most of the time. So let them talk, and they'll talk about themselves and what they are looking for.

Each time you use Hot Button salesmanship you apply imagination to your selling. This makes you not just a more creative salesperson, but a more effective one as well. More effective, because it will take you less time to close the sale once you have discovered the Hot Button of your prospect and have built your presentation around it—at least that part of the presentation needed to do the job. And do you realize how important this time factor is? Most people think that the effectiveness of a sales presentation is determined by how much is sold. Not so. The best way to evaluate a salesperson's effectiveness is by determining how long it takes that individual to close a sale. Obviously, when less time is required to close any one sale, more time is left to go out and make new ones. And Hot Button salesmanship will save you a great deal of valuable selling time.

To show you exactly how Hot Button selling works, let's assume that you are selling component parts to a manufacturing facility. You have made a good approach and are now giving the prospect a chance to talk. He tells you that he has been buying from a competitor (200 miles away) and is satisfied with the product. He also mentions that because deliveries are sometimes slow, he finds himself overstocking to insure that production is never held up. He has already given you his Hot Button: *avoidance of down time.* (In manufacturing this is a very costly problem.) Now you swing into Hot Button selling. Instead of covering all of your product's benefits as you usually do, go over the most important one for the moment. Then hit his Hot Button by saying, "With my product, Mr. Jones, you can stop worrying about down time. Since our distributor is located only ten miles from here (assuming that this is true) you can count on twenty-four-hour service. And I routinely see that the distributor is always well-stocked."

That's how you capitalize on this prospect's dominant desire. Each time you are able to bring *avoidance of down time* into your presentation you are hitting his Hot Button and getting that much closer to making the sale. Incidentally, his secondary Hot Button was his displeasure in having to *overstock.* Mentioning the removal of this problem at opportune places in your presentation would have afforded still another example of creative, Hot Button selling.

CREATIVE PRESENTATIONS ARE ORGANIZED PRESENTATIONS

A creative salesperson uses as much imagination as possible in organizing a sales presentation. And it certainly should be organized. Forget this business of "playing it by ear." You will be out of tune. All systematized, creative salespeople know the value of an organized presentation. You can join their ranks without delay. First you'll need a formula that gives structure to your presentation; then you simply proceed in your own words, plugging in the product knowledge that you already have. In the process you will be amazed at your own resourcefulness.

Five Reactions You Can't Do Without

Let's begin with your organizational formula. The most effective one known begins with the premise that there are certain reactions that must take place in the minds of your prospects in order for you to make a sale. These reactions are like road marks. After all, each time you start out to make a sale you begin a trip over a strange road that winds in and out of the subconscious mind of your prospect. Your destination is the prospect's Hot Button. The road marks along the way are reactions that you must get—and in the right sequence.

First of all, your prospects must decide to **listen.** And they must do this with their minds as well as their ears. Only then can they **absorb** what you are saying. Then your prospects have to **believe** your statements in order to accept them. After that, they must be able to see how your proposition **applies** to what they're trying to do. And finally, you must influence them to the degree that they're willing to **act** now. Remember: these reactions simply must take place in the minds of your prospects if you are to create a sale. You must get prospects to listen, to absorb, to believe, to apply, and to act.

If this seems to you like an almost impossible task, stop thinking that way. You positively can influence the prospect's thinking in order to bring about these reactions. You can virtually lay a track on which the interview will run, enabling you to exercise full control. That track will consist of answers to five questions. These five questions are on the minds of every one of your prospects, often so deeply imbedded that the questions are never asked outright. But they are there, nevertheless, and they must be answered if you are to make your sale. If you can provide convincing answers to these questions, you will succeed in eliciting the five reactions we've just discussed. But should you leave even one of these questions unanswered, you make it necessary for your prospects to dig for answers on their own. And this is something a prospect will rarely do.

The Five W's

Here, then, are the five questions. Note how they not only coincide with the reactions we've been discussing, but also how they complete the formula into which you can plug your product knowledge and come up with a creative presentation.

The first question is *"Why?"* Whenever you come on the scene, your prospects immediately wonder, "Why should I take the time to listen to this salesperson's presentation?" The best way to answer this is to give them a quick glimpse of the end result you can produce for them if they let you tell the rest of your story. Do this effectively and you will gain their interest and complete attention. If, for example, you were to say, "My machine will save you $100,000 a year," their ears would perk up, their eyes widen, and they'd want to hear all about your machine because the end result is of great interest to them.

The second question is, *"What is it?"* Many people who sell like to keep the prospect in suspense. They spend far too much time leading up to what the product or service actually is. Instead of increasing the curiosity level, however, this technique can arouse impatience or even antagonize the prospect. The better technique is to slide into a crisp description of your product as soon as you've given a quick glimpse of the end result it can produce. A good prospect is usually busy, and will greatly appreciate your getting quickly to the point and saving time for everyone.

The next question is, *"Who says so?"* Here is where the name of your company comes in. Also, at this point, you produce printed material that backs up your statements. Just because you make certain claims is no reason for your prospect to believe them. Credibility is always a problem in selling. A few dishonest salespeople making the rounds have spoiled it for the army of honest ones. So always be ready to produce literature—reprints of articles, ads, newspaper clippings, or anything *in print* that repeats what you are saying. By doing so you erase from the prospect's mind any doubt that may have been there. People tend to place greater trust in the printed word. Probably this is because they assume that most companies wouldn't print an outright lie and risk a possible lawsuit.

The fourth question is, *"Who did it?"* The prospect wants to know who has used your product or service and was pleased with the results obtained. This question can be a virtual gold mine in selling. Nothing works more consistently than the use of testimonial letters that give praise to you and what you sell. Many salespeople overlook this aspect of a presentation—often because they don't have any testimonial letters to show. Well, such letters are not hard to get. If you are new with a company, ask another member of the sales staff for copies of any testimonial letters being used. Even if they were addressed to another salesperson, it doesn't matter. You are selling the very same thing. Later, as you produce sales and develop satisfied customers, be sure to get letters of your own. It's especially easy to do at the opportune moment. When buyers go out of their way to pay you a compliment or praise your product, look them in the eye and say, "I really appreciate your kindnesses, and you have no idea how helpful it would be to me if you would put what you just said in writing." You will be most surprised at how willingly your request will be granted. And, obviously, the larger and more important the company your buyer represents, the more valuable such a letter will become in your presentation.

Finally, the prospect wants to know *"What do I get?"* This is where you add it all up. This is actually the close. You have been hitting the prospect's Hot Button throughout the presentation. You have been stressing all of the benefits that apply to this person's dominant concern. When you sum it all up for the prospect, you are restating all of the benefits as they relate to the Hot Button that you uncovered early in the conversation.

This is what the five-W presentation is all about. You organize a presentation that answers each of these questions:

1. **W**hy?
2. **W**hat is it?
3. **W**ho says so?
4. **W**ho did it?
5. **W**hat do I get?

And this is how it all works. When you answer the question *"Why?"* your prospects decide to *listen* and you have reached their ears. Once you answer the question *"What is it?"* they are able to *absorb* and understand your idea. Now you move into the subconscious mind by answering the question *"Who says so?"* When you do, they'll see that there is responsibility behind your promises and they'll *believe* your statements. Your answer to the question *"Who did it?"* gives them something to *apply* to what they're trying to accomplish themselves, and you've passed another milestone. And when you answer the question *"What do I get?"* the sale is complete. They decide to *act.* You are right on target. All that's needed now is a connection between that Hot Button in their minds and their mouths. They tell you, "Okay," and out comes the sale.

This five-W formula is what brings creative sales into existence. It has increased the salaries and incomes of tens of thousands of salespeople. Many businesses have installed this formula from top to bottom in every branch of their business, and have become the leaders in their industry. Anyone who has made the effort to organize a presentation using these five w's has been repaid a thousand fold.

Write It Out

Here is a most important suggestion. Write out your entire presentation using the five-W formula. Make sure that each of the five questions is answered thoroughly as part of your presentation. In the process, look over the wording very carefully. Take out weak words and replace them with strong ones. Make certain that you use good, descriptive adjectives to paint word-pictures for you. And now you have a completely organized presentation.

Give this five-W presentation pattern the toughest test you possibly can. Present it to the toughest possible buyers. You will be delighted at how much you will have added to your selling power. Once it has proved itself to you, then you are ready to use it on every single sales interview. Your sales curve is bound to be influenced—upwards.

CREATIVITY: A WAY OF BEING

By mastering the use of the five-W presentation, you do not automatically become as creative as you need to be in selling. Far from it. Creativity is something you must strive for and develop on a daily basis, from now on. Building a creative mind is much like building a muscle. The more you exercise it, the more it develops. And you should look for ways to think creatively even when you're not selling.

The reason why most people don't think creatively is because they accept the obvious. They accept generalities. Sayings that have been around for decades are accepted as fact. Yet such sayings are not always necessarily true. Suppose, for instance, that you are riding along the highway and you pass a restaurant. The parking lot is filled to capacity. Someone in your car says, "Look at that crowded parking lot. The food must be great." Everyone else in the car agrees. The creative thinker wouldn't accept that. Why does the food have to be good? Maybe it's senior citizens' night at greatly reduced prices. Maybe there's a wedding reception and the father of the bride got a good deal at six dollars per person. Maybe it's bingo night in the downstairs function room. The possibilities are endless.

And speaking of food, here is one generality that I've been hearing for years: "Roadside diners have the best food. Truck drivers always eat there, and they know where to find good food while on the highways." Some years back, as a salesman on the road, I checked this out. The statement is false. Most roadside diners dish out slop disguised as food. A peek in the kitchen is enough to make you lose your appetite. I was convinced that the local boards of health should have closed down most of them. And the reason that truck drivers eat at diners is not because they are gourmets. I discovered that it's because there is always enough surrounding land for them to park their trucks. So, another generality down the drain.

Do you believe *all* signs—the ones that say "final sale," or "no refunds," or "no ticket, no laundry?" As a creative thinker, you'll decide that exceptions can and will be made. They usually are, for people like you who test the strength of such edicts.

I'm sure that you get the idea. Force yourself to think creatively not only while you are selling, but all the time. Soon it becomes an interesting game. And you can always make a game of it. At your next cocktail party, for example, pass out paper and pencil to your guests and ask them to list twenty-five uses for string, for a shoe box, or a napkin ring. At first your guests will become quiet as they think of practical uses. When the practical possibilities have run out you will begin to hear giggling. They will now be reaching for more far-out uses, and some will be quite comical—especially when all read their papers aloud. It's a game, but also a tremendous exercise in creative thinking.

One of the best lessons in creativity is absolutely free and available to you, on a daily basis, in your own home and during your leisure hours. What do you do when a commercial appears on your television screen? Do you go to the refrigerator for another beer? Or to the lav? Or engage in conversation to kill the minute or so that the commercial takes? If so, you may be letting thousands of extra sales slip through your fingers. You should be analyzing those commercial messages by asking yourself, "Who are they trying to reach? Why are they saying it that way? Did they prove their claims? Did they ask for the order?" Just remember that sponsors pay as much as $250,000 for a one-minute TV commercial. That's a lot of money for one quick message. And think of the creative people in ad agencies who are paid handsomely to come up with those TV commercials. The reason they are paid so well is because their creative talents generate sales—and lots of them. You can absorb a great deal of their creativity by scrutinizing their work, which is beamed at you constantly.

Decide today that you will become more creative than you ever thought possible. If you agree that creative selling will increase your selling power and your income, then you will constantly strive to think creatively. Make absolutely certain that all of your sales interviews are organized according to the five-W presentation formula. You will be delighted at your creativity—and even more delighted at the additional sales which you will enjoy.

CREATIVITY CHECKLIST

	Always	Some-times	Never
I find myself acting as a leader.	☐	☐	☐
I revise my sales presentation to make it better.	☐	☐	☐
I build a sales presentation around the prospect's "Hot Button."	☐	☐	☐
Whenever I revise my presentation I write it out.	☐	☐	☐
My sales presentation is based on the five w's.	☐	☐	☐
I look for ways to think creatively.	☐	☐	☐
When something is obvious I accept it.	☐	☐	☐
I analyze commercials on TV and radio as an exercise in creativity.	☐	☐	☐
Creative games intrigue me.	☐	☐	☐
I attempt creative tasks.	☐	☐	☐

Note: See Appendix section for correct answers.

five

TIME-TESTED SELLING TECHNIQUES

An important quality of successful salespeople is a thorough understanding of what they are doing. Strangely enough, many salespeople lack this complete awareness. Certainly they know that they are selling, they know well the product or service to be sold, and they meet with a reasonable amount of success. But ask them to define exactly what they do when they are selling—to break down into specific steps the selling process that they use—and the answers you will get won't make much sense.

There is no question that selling is, in part, a psychological process. This does not mean, however, that each sales call should become a psychological tug of war in which the stronger and more glib contestant ends up the winner. Far from it. Like other professions, selling can and should be practiced exactingly, methodically, and with a complete, step-by-step understanding. Think for a moment of how far away you would stay from a physician who had a reputation for practicing medicine by trial and error.

75

THE THREE PARTS OF ANY SALE

Let's begin with the fundamental principle that no matter what you sell—be it a product or service—there will always be three parts to any sale. These are known as the **approach,** the **demonstration**, and the **close**. When people who have never had any formal sales training are asked, "Which of these is the most important?" invariably the answer is, "The close." They will be quick to rationalize that if you don't close the sale you have nothing. How wrong that thinking is. In the approach, we get the interest of a prospect. In the demonstration (or presentation) we convince prospects that what we have is best for them. And in the close, we persuade them to take action *now*. It follows, therefore, that the approach will always be the most important part of any sale. After all, how can you close an individual without first obtaining that person's interest? You will see this clearly just as soon as we analyze exactly what happens in each of these three parts of the sale.

The Attention-Getting Approach

Not only is the approach the most important part of any sale, but the first thirty seconds are crucial. No approach can succeed unless something very specific happens in those first thirty seconds. It is known as neutralizing the prospect's mind. You see, the fact that you have arrived on the scene is no reason why your prospects should stop thinking about their own concerns and start considering yours. Obviously, then, your approach must be so well-planned that it neutralizes your prospects' minds almost instantly and starts them thinking in the direction you planned.

Unfortunately, most salespeople do not have an approach, per se. They think that they do, but what they actually use is an extremely weak substitute. Here is a typical approach used by most salespeople during those important thirty seconds:

"Good morning, Ms. Jones, my name is Bill Smith. I'm from the ABC Company and I came here to tell you about my newest product." The prospect, however, is not particularly interested in your name, especially if you are not even known to each other. To open with, "My name is . . ." is so weak that it's useless. We have already said that the approach must gain immediate attention. Your name will not do that. What you need is an approach that immediately intrigues the imaginations of your prospects, grasps their interest, and neutralizes their minds. Only then do you have an interested and open mind that can be sold.

If you work for a company whose policy demands that all sales representatives open their sales interviews by introducing themselves and the company name, then obviously you must follow that policy. But after you have done so, you can still swing into an approach that will neutralize the prospect's mind. Naturally, it is better if you can reverse the order, but policies must be followed—that's fundamental. If you are not bound by such a policy, I suggest that you begin with an approach that will arrest the attention of your prospects rather than with a recitation of names. This does not mean, of course, that you must remain incognito. Of course you're going to tell prospects who you are and what company you represent. But it simply doesn't come first if you want to make the biggest impression and gain their interest.

To neutralize the prospect's mind and gain interest at the same time, you can use any of three methods. One of them is based on *curiosity*, another on *prospect* (or customer) *interest*, and a third on *appreciation*. Decide today to be completely different from most of the other people who sell. Develop a substantial number of approaches and rehearse them so that you'll be able to use them comfortably and in a smooth, flowing fashion. You will be amazed at the results.

Arouse their curiosity.   Of these three approaches, the one based on curiosity is by far the most effective. We all know that most people are curious. They always want to know what's going on or what is meant by a specific phrase. Why not capitalize on this by using a curiosity-arousing approach that makes the prospect *want to know more*. An excellent way of doing this is to give your product or service a different name—one that makes sense when you explain it, but which no one else has ever heard before. One very successful salesman called his product a "health machine." Invariably his prospects asked, "What's a health machine?" (Their minds had been instantly neutralized.) Then he would explain: "It's a bicycle that goes nowhere. You pedal it just for exercise, which keeps you physically fit and healthy. That's why I call it a health machine." His prospects would smile, understand and be intrigued—and this salesperson would proceed to close his sale.

When you first give your product a new name, you may feel slightly uncomfortable. The startled looks you'll get from prospects when they say, "What are you talking about?" may bother you, make you feel like an oddball. Discard that feeling immediately. Rejoice in the fact that your approach has worked. You have successfully neutralized their minds. And as a result, you are now working on minds that have been properly conditioned to be sold.

Some salespeople resist changing their ways with the excuse that using such a technique is impossible in their industries because it's far too gimmicky. Forget that kind of reasoning. Some of the largest, most dignified corporations use this technique not only in their personal selling efforts, but in their advertising as well. Not long ago, for example, IBM ran a sixteen-page insert in tabloid form in the Sunday *New York Times*, a rather expensive piece of advertising. The front cover revealed nothing more than an enlarged face of a man with the phrase, "The Mind Extender," inscribed across his forehead. The back cover was exactly the same. To find out what a "mind extender" was, you had no choice but to turn to the inside pages. When you did, you discovered that it was an IBM computer. How many people do you think would have looked inside if the cover had been captioned, "Guess What's New

With IBM Computers?" Other large companies have also taken advantage of the renaming technique. Beechcraft, which promotes airplanes for corporate use, calls one of its planes a "multiplying machine." (When you read the ad copy you discover that buying a corporate plane enables you to *multiply* your executives immediately, because they can be in more places in less time.) And the John Deere Company calls its riding lawn mower a "weekend freedom machine."

You see, the giant companies do it. Why can't you? You simply must adjust your thinking and not feel uncomfortable when using a curiosity-arousing approach. And, when done right, with some creative thinking on your part, you can get the attention and intrigue the imagination of just about everybody. I remember a day when I was driving along a New York expressway and found myself tailing a truck with the warning, "Caution! Blind Man Driving" painted in large letters on its rear doors. The mystery was cleared up when I passed the truck and saw the lettering on its side panel, which read: "Quality Venetian Blind Company."

Stimulate prospect interest.   When using the second type of approach, based on customer or prospect interest, you give the prospect a quick glimpse of the end result. You open with statements such as, "In just a few minutes I can show you how your overhead can be cut by at least 15%," or, "Your shipping expenses will be cut in half." There are very few people who won't want to listen to more of your story after an opening like that. But you can make it even more dramatic if you work at it.

Let's suppose that you are selling a piece of equipment to industry which will cut down production costs. Assume that your equipment will bring about a savings (according to their production, which you have estimated) of approximately $200 a week. That's $10,400 per year. You walk in, look the prospect right in the eye and, while shaking hands, you say pleasantly, "Good morning, Mr. Jones, I came here today to give you $10,400." The normal response will be, "How are you going to do that?" And you're off with your presentation. The prospect may kid around with you and ask if you're going to give him a check or cold, hard cash. But that's fine. A little levity never hurts in selling. The important thing is that the prospect is "with you" and very willing to hear the rest of your story.

Show your appreciation.   The third approach is based on the premise that everybody likes to be appreciated. This type of approach gets people to like you. It does not mean that you flatter them, because flattery is insincere; it's a form of lying. And we have already said that truly professional salespeople will never tell lies. To use an approach based on appreciation, you merely remark favorably and truthfully on something you like about a person. For instance, you can appreciate a man's tie by commenting on its color or design. You can appreciate a woman's hairdo, the color of her dress, or the flowers on her desk. You can appreciate an executive's office that has just been redecorated with new drapes and furniture. Or you can appreciate the remodeling job done on a retail store, particularly if you are talking to its owner. All you need do is walk in and say nothing else except, "This is beautiful. You did a marvelous job of redecorating. Your customers will love this." Your prospects may not even know you but they'll love you for it. Chances are they've spent a barrel of money for a remodeling effort that far too few customers have bothered to comment on.

All three types of approaches are effective. But make no mistake about the fact that the one based on curiosity is the most effective. People get stimulated when their imaginations have been intrigued. To stimulate means to create interest, and that's what we're trying to accomplish with any approach. From now on, start every single sales interview by shaking hands and using a well-planned approach. You must know exactly what your approach will be before you get anywhere near the prospect you are about to call on. Far too many people who sell give very little thought, or no thought at all, to the approach. If you were to ask any salesperson about to

make a sales call what his or her first few sentences were going to be, chances are you'd hear, "I don't know. I'll play it by
ear." That's how much importance is generally given to the
approach. The things that are said are usually plucked out of
thin air, and often they are meaningless.

You might say, "Not me. I think about what I say." Well,
how about doing a little soul searching? How many times in
the course of the day do you say, upon meeting someone, "Hi,
how are you?" As you say that, are you really concerned about
that person's general health? And even if you are, is it your job
to go around and check on the physical well-being of people,
or is it to get through to them and sell your product or service? The next time you happen to be in a retail store when a
salesperson comes in to see the owner or manager, make it a
point to stand within hearing distance and listen to the beginning of their conversation. It can almost be guaranteed that
you will hear the following:

"Hi, Jane, how are you?"
"Fine, Bill, and you?"
"Fine."
"How have you been?"
"Great—and you?"
"Fine."
"How's everything?"
"Fine, and how's everything with you?"
"Fine."

What does this exchange really mean? The explanation is simple: two people came face to face; one of them, the salesperson, was unprepared with an approach; and, not knowing
what to say to each other, they engaged in the usual meaningless small talk.

As of today, resign from the how-are-you association. Assume that the people that you meet are well. (After all, if they
weren't, they'd be at home or in a hospital.) If others jump the

gun and say, "How are you?" come back with, "Nice to see you." And mean it. Start using such phrases as:

"Nice to be with you"
"Great to be in your company"
"It's a pleasure to see you"
"Nice to hear your voice" (when on the phone)

Warm statements like these are much more meaningful and make people feel better than the automatic, "How are you?" It all boils down to the necessity of becoming more aware of what we say at all times, but particularly during the approach. Our words constantly produce an effect on others. In selling, that effect must be thought out in advance. The right words used at the right time make for professionalism in selling. Superfluous, meaningless words place the ineptness of salespeople on display.

The Convincing Demonstration

The actual convincing process comes into play in the second part of any sale, the demonstration. But don't assume that this is solely a physical act. The word *demonstration* is used in a psychological sense as well. In the demonstration, you convince prospects that you have the best product or service that they can use to fill the needs uncovered in the approach. It is in the demonstration that you put forth the benefits of your product or service in such a powerful manner that they sink in and sell. And you must make certain that you demonstrate the full value and importance of *all* the benefits of your product or service, because it is in the demonstration that the sale is actually made. Not in the close, as so many people think. You see, since the actual convincing is done in the demonstration, it is here that the prospect decides to buy (or not to buy). Assuming that your demonstration is handled properly and that the prospect has been convinced, the close becomes simply a matter of how the deal will be consummated—rather than whether or not it will be.

Surprisingly enough, every single demonstration produces a sale. That's right. Either you sell your prospects or they sell you the idea that they have been getting along without you very well and don't need what you're selling now. In other words, the best salesperson always wins. A sale is always made, one way or the other. Most salespeople go into a demonstration in the worst possible way. They unload a barrage of statements—a rapid-fire, unorganized recitation of the features of the products or services they sell. They go on and on, hoping that at some point during their dissertation the prospect will say something like, "I can see how I can use your product, so let's write the order." Rarely, however, will prospects interrupt you to say, "I will buy." What usually happens under these circumstances is that prospects will let you complete your entire story, and then give you some reason why they can't use your product or service.

A convincing demonstration will hit, as often as possible, upon the prospect's Hot Button. Every time that you bring out a feature, you should follow it up with a benefit. Here's a simple example. If you were selling a chair to a prospect, you *could* recite all of its features: the kind of wood used, how it was imported, how it was handmade by skilled craftsmen, and the quality control procedures used. But the prospect wants to know more about the benefits than the features: is the chair comfortable, will it last long enough to justify its price, will it store easily, and will it look nice in the office. As you can see, the benefits are all related to what's in it for the prospect. And a recitation of features alone doesn't automatically translate into benefits for the prospect. If we don't make that translation, we are only doing one half of the job that needs to be done in the demonstration. That translation could be defined as the spoon-feeding of benefits to the prospect. Well, why not spoon-feed? It isn't that prospects are dumb. Most prospects today are rather astute. The reason we must spoon-feed benefits is because most people live such complicated lives that they have enough on their minds as it is. We cannot and should not expect them, in addition, to translate our features into their benefits. We must do it for them, in order to make the demonstration sink in and sell.

Make an impact.   When you build impact into your demonstration you will greatly accelerate the convincing process. How do you create impact? Well, let's talk about that for a moment. What do you suppose is the most impactful thing in the world today? Some people will say the economy, money, or taxes. Well, forget it. The most impactful thing in the world is television. Why? Because it gets you through the eyes and ears at the same time, and it is virtually impossible for your mind to wander when you are watching the tube.

Think about the last time you were driving home at the end of the week and wondered, "What's the weather going to be like this weekend?" So you turned on the radio in your car and listened to the news, thinking that you'd catch the weather forecast at the end of it. As you drove along and heard about the fires, the murders, and the accidents, your mind began to wander to that big sale you made, or the one you didn't make and why you didn't make it. Before you knew it you heard music coming from the radio speaker. And you came to the realization that you'd been listening to over ten minutes of news only to miss the weather forecast while you were preoccupied with other thoughts. At home, watching television, that can't happen. When you watch the news on the tube and the meteorologist comes on with the weather forecast, you are given not only the local forecast, but the outlook for the entire country. Now, you're not planning on spending your weekend too far from home. But there you are, your mouth slightly agape as you watch and listen to the forecast for places thousands of miles from where you will be. And do you mind doing this? Not at all. You are actually intrigued. You are being given a great deal of information and you're absorbing every bit of it. They have you by the eye and the ear at the same time.

Repeated studies have shown that people respond through the eye 87% of the time and through the ear only 7% of the time. Yet so many salespeople depend on communication through the ear—and only the ear. If you want to build impact into your demonstration you must come up with something to show. Certainly you have literature on your products or services. Most of the time such literature is very colorful and impactful. Why not use it? Some salespeople fear that the introduction of literature during the demonstration will distract the prospect from what is being said. The prospect may begin to read the literature and stop listening. To some degree that is true, but there is a way of getting around it. Don't ever give your prospects literature in the process of convincing. Instead, hold the literature just far enough away so that it would be rude for them to reach over and grab it. By pointing, direct their attention to a specific statement or photograph contained in the literature. As you do this, watch their faces for any reaction that might reveal a Hot Button you can zero in on later. Finally, having made the proper impact through the eye as well as the ear, you are ready to hand over the literature, remaining silent while they absorb the contents, and wait for questions.

Get your prospects to agree with you.   There are two things that you can do during your demonstration to pave the way for a simple and successful close. First of all, you must bear in mind that there is a psychological aspect of the convincing process which involves your prospect's unspoken agreement. It's this silent agreement that you must strive to win long before you reach the close. When the prospect has said yes throughout the presentation it is very difficult to say no at the end. This would almost represent a contradiction. First you must develop insurance against a negative response by avoiding open-ended questions which the prospect can answer with a yes or a no. Then you can practically guarantee an affirmative reaction with statements that point, incontestably, to the benefits of your product—statements like, "You will agree, Mr.

Jones, that cutting your overhead is something you want to do," or, "You will agree, Mr. Jones, that reducing your cost of raw materials will increase your profits." How could the prospect say no to statements like these? To get the full impact of this psychological technique, nod your head as you say, "And you will agree. . ." Always nod. You'll find that your prospects will nod with you. This makes it even easier for them to say yes during the close, and much harder to contradict themselves.

There is one other way in which you can make the close easier during the demonstration: assume that the sale will be made and act accordingly. I emphasize the word *assume*. Naturally, all through life, you have heard that you must assume nothing. Well, forget that when it comes to selling. Because when you assume from the very beginning of the interview that you will make the sale, your attitude will be different and so will your vocabulary. When you expect the prospect to buy, you use much more enthusiasm, your manner is much more positive, your personality is at its most compelling, and the prospect is influenced by your confidence. Under these circumstances your vocabulary follows right in line. You'll never use negative words, which so many of us interject in our regular conversation. Neither will you make qualifying statements like this one: "If you buy this product, Mr. Jones, you will find . . ." That small "if" lets your prospects know that you're not really confident that they're going to buy. Instead you will say, "As soon as you put my product into use, you will find. . ." This statement conveys your complete confidence in making the sale. Remove all negative words from your vocabulary—words like *would, should, could, can, maybe,* and *perhaps*. You should be using the word *will* instead. One of the worst qualifying phrases is, "I think." When you tell your prospect, "I think you will find my product to be most satisfactory," you are really saying, "I am not sure." When you "think," you don't "know." As a professional salesperson, you should know your product well and know exactly what it will do. You must not be wishy-washy about anything that you sell. Look at it this way. If you needed surgery and your doctor told you, "I think this kind of operation might be successful," would you stick around to find out?

The Professional Close

The third part of any sale, *the close,* is often the most difficult one for salespeople. There is probably more misunderstanding about the close than about anything else connected with selling. Even after years in the profession, many people who sell still regard the close as that part of the sale when you practically have to get prospects down on their backs, twist their arms, and crush them into submission. That notion is ridiculous. We have already seen how the close can be set up and simplified during the demonstration process. Some people make it hard for themselves, however, and that's when pressure always comes into the act. Some people say, "In my business you simply can't use any pressure whatsoever. I'm in an industry where it's strictly the soft sell that pays off." Well, we know that's wrong, because if you don't use *some* pressure you will get only the easy sales. Still others in sales work will say, "In my business you must use a great deal of pressure. You practically have to hit the prospect over the head in order to make the sale." But that's wrong too. You can use so much pressure that you not only lose the sale, you also lose the prospect—forever. People resent high pressure and will avoid being on the receiving end. So when you use high pressure you risk losing both the sale and the customer at the same time.

The objective of the close is clear-cut. You are trying to do one thing and one thing alone: to get your prospects to express the decision that they made during the demonstration. Remember? It was there that you did the convincing. And while inevitably some pressure must be applied, it must be done most professionally.

You probably already know about high and low pressure and the difference between each kind. But I've found it extremely helpful to define pressure in terms of two different types. One of them I call **acceptable pressure** and the other **offensive pressure**. Acceptable pressure is the kind that you apply when the thought that's uppermost in your mind is what you can do for your prospects. As long as you are genuinely trying to see that your prospects benefit from your product or service—as long as you keep putting your prospects in center stage by dramatically describing what's in it for them—you are using acceptable pressure. People will rarely object to that type of pressure because you are talking about them, and they like that. Offensive pressure, on the other hand, has quite the opposite effect. Offensive pressure is the kind that you apply when the thought that's uppermost in your mind is what you are going to get out of making the sale. You are thinking of your commission. You probably already have it spent. And this type of pressure always shows. It becomes quite clear to the prospect that you are trying to make the sale for your own personal gain. The prospect resents it. Without question you will find that using acceptable pressure, along with the closing techniques you have developed, will make closing a lot easier for you.

Ask more than once.   Regardless of how refined your closing techniques may be, their effectiveness is always related to how many times you ask for the order. Many people fail to realize that asking for the order once is rarely enough. It's ample, of course, when the prospect buys on your very first attempt at closing. But when you know that the road to the sale has been bumpy all along, closing becomes not just a matter of asking for the order, but of how many times you will ask for it. After spending years studying the experiences of salespeople in a variety of industries, we have come to the conclusion that you must ask for the order *a minimum of three times*. And *five times* is better still. This may sound like a lot, but there is good reason for it. A survey on closing attempts conducted at Notre

Dame University revealed that 46% of the participants asked for the order once and then quit; 24% asked for the order twice; 14% asked for the order three times; and 12% asked for the order four times. Yet the very same survey showed that 60% of the acceptances came on the fifth attempt.

Now you can see why five times is better. Not until you have asked a fifth time have you given yourself a shot at that 60% chance of hearing a yes. Naturally, the five requests that you make for an order will be interspersed with other parts of your presentation. And they won't all necessarily come during one call, either. This is how it all works. At the opportune time in your sales presentation, you ask for the order a first time. If you don't get a yes, you go back to selling with the emphasis on the benefits. Now you ask a second time. Still no sale? Then go back and sell more benefits. You ask a third time and, if you don't get the order, you leave. At this point you write a note to the prospect explaining that you neglected to mention a benefit of special interest during your call; you describe the benefit and ask for the order again. That makes four. Then you wait a few days for the note to arrive. Finally you phone the prospect, ask if the note was received, slide in still another benefit, and ask for the order again. That's five.

On several occasions I have been on speaking programs with Victor Borge, the famed comedian who is also an accomplished pianist. He always tells this story: "My great grandfather invented a soft drink. He called it One-Up and it didn't sell. The following year he changed it to Two-Up. It still didn't sell. Each year he kept changing the name and when it was called Six-Up, he died. If he had only known." If salespeople only realized that 60% of the acceptances come on the fifth attempt at closing, they would never consider asking for the order any less than five times.

"Ask and you shall receive." Certainly you've heard that phrase many times before, and you've agreed with it. Why not adopt it? People think a lot more of you when you have the courage to ask for something. If you skirt around the issue, they think less of you. As a professional salesperson you must become a very strong closer. You do this by studying good closing techniques, and by training yourself to ask for the order at the right time, in the right way, and as many as five times. It's wonderful to have pride and it's great to be everybody's friend. But to bring home the bacon on a regular basis demands that you know how to close. It demands that you have the courage to ask. If there was ever a secret for survival, this is it.

Before you sell others, sell yourself.   There must be a good reason why almost fifty percent of the people who sell ask for the order only once. I believe strongly that the reason is because they are not sold tightly on their own propositions. Consequently, they don't find it proper to push beyond a certain point. How do you feel about the product or service you sell? Do you believe that it's a good proposition that you are presenting to people, day in and day out? If not, you have some strong self-convincing to do. And I want to help you with that.

First of all, look at what you sell from the standpoint of returns and cost. Your object is to magnify the first and minimize the second. Suppose that you are selling a piece of equipment which will save a company approximately $100 a month. To magnifying the returns, think in terms of yearly rather than monthly savings. Tell your prospect that the saving is $1,200 a year, $6,000 in five years, or $12,000 in ten years (depending on the life of the piece of equipment). These figures are a lot more impressive than the smaller figure of $100 a month, and you are not lying. People react favorably to large savings, and they usually lack the imagination to figure out the total savings for themselves.

Now look at your proposition from the standpoint of minimizing cost. If you are selling a piece of equipment which costs $350 and will last for at least one year, you might say, "Mr. Jones, this machine is yours for less than a dollar a day." Here again, you are not lying. There are 365 days in the year, and the price of the machine is $350—isn't that less than one dollar a day?

So now you have a large figure to give the prospect in the way of a benefit, and a small figure to make it easy for the prospect to buy. Take paper and pencil right now and develop these figures for the product or service you sell. In doing so, you'll gain the conviction you need to go out and ask for the order a lot more than one time. And the figures you develop will certainly be useful when closing.

Still another way you can sell yourself on what you have to offer is by referring to the price of your product or service as an investment rather than a cost. The cost of just about everything we buy can be looked upon as an investment. It's simply a case of how we think. And, as a professional salesperson, you are constantly influencing people's thinking. Your prospects will think of price in terms of cost as long as you let them think that way. But if you are consistent in referring to the price as an investment throughout your entire sales presentation, you can make them think differently and improve your closing techniques at the same time. The investment makes a lot of sense. A cost is something to be considered from a budgetary standpoint, and its size is always of consequence. Generally speaking, buyers have the attitude that salespeople cost them money. Many a buyer has been quoted as saying, when things are tight, "This week I won't see any salespeople and save some money." Look over your written presentation carefully. Make certain that you delete from your vocabulary the word *cost* and replace it with the word *investment*.

SELLING TECHNIQUES CHECKLIST

	Always	Some-times	Never
I begin a sales call with a planned approach.	☐	☐	☐
Curiosity-arousing approaches seem to work for me.	☐	☐	☐
Gimmicky attention-getting techniques bother me.	☐	☐	☐
When using an approach based on prospect interest, I give the buyer a quick glimpse of the end result.	☐	☐	☐
My approaches based on appreciation may contain flattery.	☐	☐	☐
I shake hands during the approach.	☐	☐	☐
Upon meeting people I'm apt to say, "How are you?"	☐	☐	☐
I translate features into benefits for prospects.	☐	☐	☐
During a presentation I ask questions that produce a yes.	☐	☐	☐
I assume that I will get an order at each sales call.	☐	☐	☐

Throughout my presen-
tation I avoid the use of
negative words and
qualifying statements.

I ask for the order at
least three times.

I minimize the price
and magnify the re-
turns.

In my presentation I use
the word *investment* in-
stead of the word *cost*.

Note: See Appendix section for correct answers.

six

DON'T BE OVERRULED BY OBJECTIONS

At some time or other you must have dealt with a very sensitive individual. Being fully aware of that person's sensitivity, you made it a point not to say the wrong thing at any one time. You knew that if the conversation didn't follow the right course, the outcome could be disastrous. So you used carefully chosen words and phrases designed to keep your sensitive friend in the right frame of mind. In fact, you said things that you knew would be readily accepted.

The most sensitive part of selling is that point in the sale when you are placed in the position of having to overcome an objection. And it happens on a regular basis. This is where, like dealing with your friend, you must say things that you know will be readily accepted. Just when you think that your most convincing demonstration has hit its mark and that you can now apply the close best suited to this situation, what happens? The prospect comes up with an objection—one which usually seems to have been pulled out of thin air. So now you have a very sensitive situation on your hands, and it separates the professionals from the amateurs in selling. If you handle the objection properly, you can still make that sale. Handle it poorly and you will lose the sale, all by yourself. Objections can frequently be a source of great difficulties in selling, but only if you are not equipped with the knowledge required to overcome them in a professional way.

One of the major reasons why people who sell find objections hard to handle is that they keep themselves so tightly sold on their propositions that no one can unsell them. (This is a very different matter from maintaining a healthy conviction that your proposition is a good one.) The slightest disparaging remark against the product or service raises the blood pressure. They believe so strongly in what they are selling that the minute an objection comes up they almost take it personally. They simply won't allow the prospect to say anything that downgrades the proposition in any way. Such loyalty may be most commendable, but it works against you. You must remain flexible in your thinking at all times. You must be able to see the prospect's viewpoint and take it in stride. This is not to say that you must agree with whatever you hear in the way of an objection. If you were to do that you would lose sales on a constant basis. What is important here is to understand exactly what's going on, make the right moves at the right time, and get back to closing the sale.

WHAT IS AN OBJECTION?

At the outset, let's clearly understand what constitutes an objection. Many salespeople like to define it, in a most positive way, as "a request for more information." Well, that's one way of getting a handle on it, but it really doesn't define an objection. Basically, an objection is a reason why a prospect can't or won't do business with you. That's what it all boils down to. You might just as well accept it and learn the best techniques to use in overcoming objections. The better you become at this, the more sales you will close. In fact, it has been said that the best closing techniques will only work when the overcoming of objections can be handled properly.

Don't let them wait. When an objection comes up, you must handle it immediately, right on the spot. Never say anything like, "We'll get to that later," or, "You'll change your mind after you've heard the rest of my presentation." Under these circumstances the prospect wonders why you won't answer the objection, and for the remainder of your presentation the prospect's mind remains preoccupied, speculating on what your motives might be. You are not working on an open, clear mind, a mind that can be sold. Besides, the longer you make prospects wait for your answer, the bigger the objection becomes in their minds. It may grow to such proportions that when you do answer it, your reasoning will be accepted only grudgingly—if at all.

Here's an example. Think about your younger days when you borrowed the family car to go to a party. You were told to be home by midnight. You agreed. You left the party in time to make good your promise but you found a flat tire on the car. Replacing it with the spare took longer than usual, and then you discovered that the spare had no air in it. Finally you arrived home, at two in the morning. By that time your parents were livid. Their imaginations had run rampant. They not only pictured you in a serious accident, but were on the verge of calling the police to get details, or calling the hospitals to find out if you had been admitted. Their nerves were very much on edge. Had you phoned them when you discovered the flat tire and explained that you would be late due to the circumstances, your arrival at that late hour would have been taken much more easily. The whole situation would not have been blown out of proportion. You see, you made them wait for an explanation.

Make it a rule to answer objections without delay. Even if an objection comes up in the very beginning of your presentation, you must stop at that very point and overcome it. Having done so, you might as well get something else straightened out. Ask if this is the prospect's only objection. If the answer is yes, you have most likely set the stage for the remainder of your demonstration. But should it happen that every time you overcome an objection the prospect follows with another, less reasonable one, there is a message here. The prospect has already decided not to buy no matter what you do. When this becomes obvious, it's time to leave and not waste any more valuable selling time.

THREE TYPES OF OBJECTIONS

Objections fall into three categories, depending upon their severity. They consist of either **viewpoints, opinions,** or **prejudices,** and each must be handled accordingly.

The Viewpoint

A viewpoint usually consists of a broad generality which the prospect doesn't really mean. For instance, you may hear a viewpoint such as, "But we have always used the ABC Company as our supplier for such products." Most likely there have been other suppliers along the way for one reason or another. And there is usually no written contract that binds the prospect to doing business solely with ABC. In other words, it's a habit that has developed over time. Given enough reason, that habit could be changed—if not entirely, then certainly to some extent.

The first step is to avoid conflict of any kind. The best way to do this is to give prospects due respect for their viewpoint. They are entitled to express a viewpoint any time they like. The constitution gives them that right. Who are we to take it away from them? So show respect for your prospect's viewpoint by saying, "I can understand how you feel, however ..." Obviously, there should always be a "however."

Whenever a viewpoint comes up in the course of your demonstration, there are three steps you should take:

1. Give prospects due respect for their viewpoints.
2. Activate a dominant desire by hitting a Hot Button.
3. Swing back into your demonstration and further clarify the point in question.

Most of the time that will be the end of the objection. And if you satisfy the prospect thoroughly, chances are that no further objections will come up during the sales interview. But bear in mind that some prospects simply want to show that they have their own ideas about certain things. Raising an objection gives them an opportunity to come "center stage" for a minute or two, if only to speak their minds. Once they have done so, they feel satisfied. In fact, there are instances when prospects don't even listen as you answer their objections. That tells you how unimportant some objections really are to the consummation of the sale. They might be raised simply because prospects want to get something off their chests.

The Opinion

An opinion is a more deeply seated objection. A good example of an opinion-type objection is when prospects tell you, "Your price is too high." They have given this some thought. It is not a generality. They have compared your price with that of your competitors and have come to the conclusion that yours is higher.

Here is how a machinery salesman I know overcomes this, using the Lacy techniques. He is regularly faced with this objection because the price of his product is 20% higher than that of his competition. As soon as the price objection comes up he says, "I can understand how you feel, Mr. Jones, but the $12,000 investment that you're going to make in my machine will give you a savings of $100,000 in ten years—$10,000 a year. And since we guarantee this machine for ten years, you can see how the original investment is well worth it." See what happens? First, he keeps the prospect's mind open by showing respect for his opinion. Secondly, he hits the prospect's Hot Button by telling him what he can gain over a period of time. Then he carries the prospect's incomplete reasoning to its conclusion. This prospect is only concerned with the price. He hasn't thought about what it would cost to be without this machine. So my friend the machine salesman tells him, then swings back into his presentation knowing full well that now this prospect has a much more receptive mind. His method of handling an opinion involves four steps:

1. Show respect for the opinion.
2. Activate a dominant desire by hitting a Hot Button.
3. Carry incomplete reasoning through to its conclusion.
4. Swing back into the demonstration.

Of course, you should be prepared for common objections. If you find that a particular objection comes up frequently in your interviews, include the answer to it in your actual presentation. I suggest that you do this very early in the sales interview, to avoid the objection being raised at all. Also, there will be instances when you will be able to sense, from the prospect's reasoning, that an objection is about to be voiced. In such cases it is best to answer the objection even before it comes out of the prospect's mouth. This technique eliminates negative thoughts in the process of the presentation and will impress your prospects, who will marvel at your ability to think quickly and to anticipate their objections.

A good exercise for handling objections, is to keep a list of all that come up in the course of your sales presentations. Record how often they occur and in what order. This will give you an insight into how many answers you should incorporate into your presentation. Regardless of the product or service you sell, you will find that there will be only three or four objections that come up with any frequency. Answer those before they arise, but don't bring objections up on your own if they are of the infrequent variety. Why prolong the interview and cloud the issue?

Too many salespeople are haunted by the thought of the many objections that are *bound* to come up in each presentation. This is a form of negative thinking. It is most revealing to note the results of regular surveys we have made during sales training classes. Members of the class are asked to jot down on paper the number of objections they think they will usually encounter. Most people anticipate ten. Some will go as high as fifteen or twenty. But when we ask them to actually list specific objections in their order of importance, most find it very difficult to get beyond five or six.

If the price of what you sell is higher than your competition's and you know that this objection will be raised nearly every interview, why not build in a complete and convincing answer to it early, in every single presentation. There is always a reason for a higher price. Maybe your product lasts longer because it was made better. Maybe you give a longer guarantee. Whatever the reasons, incorporate them convincingly and smoothly into your actual presentation in its very early stages. Whenever you can overcome an objection even before it rears its ugly head, you are way ahead of the game.

The Prejudice

Prejudices are the most troublesome of all objections and require special handling. A prejudice is a deep-seated hatred, loaded with animosity, which is far from easy to cope with. Here's an example. A customer is promised materials which he needs to manufacture the product he sells. The delivery date is missed by sixty days. When the delivery is finally made, he discovers that the wrong material has been sent and cannot be used. The situation costs his company a great deal of business.

He phones the supplier and gets no satisfaction. When he finally obtains the proper materials, he is then billed at a higher
rate. He is informed that during the delay the price went up.
The customer argues that the delay was not his fault, but this
gets him nowhere. Finally, in complete disgust, he pays the
bill as presented and vows that he will never do business with
that supplier again. That's how prejudices come about.

Now imagine yourself as a brand new salesperson for this
particular supplier. You are very happy about your new job
and you are proud to be associated with this great organization that you have joined. You go into the territory with tremendous enthusiasm, and you call on this past customer
without prior knowledge of the incident just described. What
do you suppose happens? In most cases, the customer becomes
incensed at your very presence. The incident may have taken
place a year or two prior to your visit, but he hasn't forgotten.
He proceeds to tear into you. He relates the incident in detail.
He gets more angry by the minute and you are in for the most
severe tongue-lashing you have ever received.

Coping with such a situation is far from pleasant, to say
the least. But if you use the right formula, time-tested over the
years, you can quickly begin the process of overcoming the
prejudice. First of all, you must let him tell you the whole
story. Don't interrupt. Hear him out—and sympathize profusely. Agree with him that he was not treated properly. Don't try
to defend your company in any way. This is one of the rare
instances when you should temporarily set aside your loyalty
to your company. Allow him to get all of this animosity out of
his system. He has been dying to do this for a long time, but he
didn't have the opportunity or the listener. When he has spent
all of his fury, has poured his heart out, say something like
this: "I can't explain how sorry I am that this happened, Mr.
Jones. Now, tell me, what do you suggest as a possible remedy
for this situation?" At first he will make demands that are far
from rational, but after more sympathizing and discussion,
these demands will become fewer and more reasonable. Usually you will not get a prejudiced customer to do business with

your company again on your very first call. You will find, though, that with each successive call the tongue-lashing becomes less severe. And, after a few calls made at relatively short intervals and properly handled, he will begin to like *you*. His animosity towards your company will begin to take a back seat to his feelings about you. When this happens, you'll be in a position to show what you can do for him and make him a customer all over again. He will listen with an open mind only after he has come to the realization that, while he's really angry with your company, he's been rather harsh to you because it wasn't your fault in the first place.

One thing must be emphasized in the handling of prejudices. In theory, any sale can be made within reason provided that you expend the necessary time and effort in bringing the sale about. However, you are the only person who can determine how much time and effort represents a good investment in overcoming a prejudice. You must determine how important this customer is to you, sales-wise; how large an order you are apt to obtain; and how much repeat business is likely to be yours. If the initial order and/or the repeat orders are not worth four, five, or six calls, then obviously to expend considerable time and effort on this antagonized customer would be unwise. Should you decide, on the other hand, that it is worth the effort to overcome the prejudice, it may be wise to make even more than six calls to correct the situation. These calls must occur no more than two to three weeks apart. If too much time elapses between calls, the reselling process is not as effective.

People are only human, and errors will always be committed. These, in turn, produce prejudices. Most of the time the errors will not be of your own making. One of many departments in your company (shipping, accounting, credit, quality control, or manufacturing) can commit an error that fosters a prejudice. Sometimes a prejudice is brought on by the mistake of the very salesperson who covered the territory just prior to your coming on the scene. Whatever the cause, the problem is now squarely in your lap and you must know how to cope with it. While it is not possible to reverse all prejudices, our research over the years has shown that as many as six out of ten can be reversed. Those numbers aren't all that bad. So, assuming that it's worth spending the time on the prejudiced company, a solid effort should be made to reverse it. Your effort should include each of the following steps:

1. Listen attentively, sympathize with the customer, and don't interrupt.
2. Ask the customer to suggest a remedy.
3. Activate a dominant desire by hitting a Hot Button.
4. Swing back into your presentation.

Naturally, it takes a great deal of will power to make repeated sales calls on prejudiced customers. Nobody likes to be on the receiving end of a tongue-lashing. No one likes to be yelled at. Look upon it as a challenge and your attitude will change substantially. You must not take the abusive treatment personally, particularly if it was not your fault to begin with. Accept the challenge for what it's worth—and it could be worth an awful lot of money to your company, as well as increased prestige for you.

Here's a technique that works very well when a prejudiced customer is shouting at you. With each reply that you are able to sneak in, lower your voice. Speak softly, and more softly each time the customer gives you an opportunity to say something. This makes the customer's shouting sound even louder than it actually is. Before long the customer will begin to feel self-conscious about shouting, particularly if there are others within hearing range, and a reversal will begin to take place. By the end of your visit you will most likely find that the customer has resumed speaking in a normal tone of voice.

When all is said and done, the most difficult part of overcoming objections is avoiding an argument. You just cannot afford the luxury of losing your temper, not ever. It doesn't matter how rude people are, or how much they antagonize you. There is simply no room for argument in selling. In fact, you must learn to accept blame that may rightfully belong to others. Always use the magic words, "I am awfully sorry." This phrase usually disarms prospects and customers. They don't hear it very often. Their attitudes will change, remarkably, because not too many people want you or anyone else to feel "awfully sorry."

Two of the greatest human virtues practiced by professional salespeople are **patience** and **tolerance**. When you are able to place yourself in the shoes of the other person, you develop the patience necessary to control your temper at all times. Tolerance should come instinctively. We have already said that if you sell, you must like people. If you like people, you will tolerate them. You will overlook their faults, their odd mannerisms, their eccentricities, and their inadequacies. How nice it is to be able to say about anybody, "We certainly don't see eye to eye, but I respect that person as a human being."

Above all, never lose sight of your goal. To professional salespeople an objection, regardless of its severity, never represents a permanent obstacle. They think of an objection as nothing more than a temporary detour. They may be slowed down briefly, but they immediately categorize the objection, handle it by using the proper formula, and then return to the convincing job at hand. Their presentation continues to flow as if no interruption had occurred, and their sights are still set on making the sale. They harbor no hard feelings or negative thoughts. They let nothing influence their effectiveness.

Constantly keep in mind that overcoming objections is always the most sensitive part of any sale. Furthermore, mishandling the sale at that point, by making even the slightest mistake, turns a possible sale into a complete disaster. If you want a rule of thumb to condition yourself in handling objections, try telling yourself, "I'm not here to win a debate, I'm here to make a sale."

OBJECTIONS CHECKLIST

	Always	Some-times	Never
Disparaging remarks against my product disturb me.	☐	☐	☐
I postpone the answering of objections until the end of the presentation.	☐	☐	☐
When an objection is voiced, I ask if it is the prospect's only objection.	☐	☐	☐
I give prospects due respect for their viewpoints and opinions.	☐	☐	☐
The answer to a frequent objection is included in my presentations.	☐	☐	☐
In overcoming objections I make it a point to hit the prospect's Hot Button.	☐	☐	☐
I will sympathize with a former customer's prejudice.	☐	☐	☐
If a prejudice cannot be overcome on the first call, I will return in the immediate future.	☐	☐	☐

Verbal attacks by
prejudiced customers
disturb me.

When a prejudiced cus-
tomer shouts, I use the
"speak softly" tech-
nique.

I am patient and toler-
ant in dealing with buy-
ers.

I will accept blame,
even when not deserved,
to keep a buyer happy.

Note: See Appendix section for correct answers.

seven

SALES STRATEGIES FOR SURVIVAL

One of the biggest problems that has always faced the outside salesperson is **waiting time.** This is the time that is literally wasted in waiting for a prospect to see you. This problem is bigger than most people realize, because waiting time is wasted time. It substantially cuts down the amount of time left for making other sales calls, materially affecting your sales production and your income.

Your survival will always be in jeopardy unless you take a substantial stand on how long you are willing to wait to obtain a sales interview with a prospect or customer. You must develop a very strong and positive attitude towards this problem and maintain it throughout your entire selling career. If there was ever an area in which attitude adjustment is a must, this is it. To waste too much time playing the waiting game is unfair to you and to your company. Depending upon the industry that you are in and how much it has cost the company to train you, keep you on the road, and subsidize your expenses, the cost of one sales call can range anywhere from fifty

109

to one-hundred-and-fifty dollars. Obviously, the only way to keep this cost down is to make as many calls as possible, and to avoid waiting time in order to do so.

THE PROSPECT WHO MAKES YOU WAIT

Many buyers rationalize that you are "just a salesperson" and that it's perfectly all right to let you wait. This is sheer disrespect for your time. There is a strategic way to handle this situation that will work in practically every instance and save you a vast amount of selling time. From now on, when you have waited for a reasonable period of time (ten to fifteen minutes and no more), step up to the receptionist or switchboard operator and say, "Will you please tell Mr. (or Ms.) Prospect that if I have come at a bad time, I will be glad to return later when he will find it more convenient to see me." When prospects receive this word it will remind them that you have been waiting, and they will either see you quickly or send back word as to how long they will be engaged. Then you can determine whether to continue to wait, to squeeze in another nearby call, or to do some telephoning. On the other hand, it may develop that seeing your prospect today isn't possible. In that case, you ask for an appointment for another day. Then, when you come in at the appointed time, you have a powerful statement to make to the receptionist. With a pleasant smile you say, "Would you please tell Mr. Prospect that Jim Smith is here for his *ten o'clock appointment.*"

Experience has shown that if you respect your own time you will gain respect for it from prospects and customers as well. They will not resent your efforts to conserve it. I have used this strategy thousands of times and have never irritated anyone by doing so. Yet it worked in just about every instance. The hours it has saved for me have been beyond calculation. The same can be true for you.

I hasten to add at this point that whenever time is spent waiting—even ten or fifteen minutes of it—make sure that it is utilized fruitfully. Don't read the old magazines that are always found in a reception area or a waiting room. Usually they're anywhere from three months to one year old. Instead, why not spend that time reading anything that will help you do a better selling job. Since salesmanship is a subject that must be studied and restudied, and since it involves your livelihood, never lose your thirst for knowledge on this subject, or for reviewing techniques which you may not have used lately. There are at least a dozen companies that produce all kinds of materials, some of them pocket-sized, that salespeople can utilize for this purpose.*

Here is a good exercise. For the next month, keep a record somewhere, perhaps in your little expense booklet, of how much waiting time you spent on every single call. When you total it and determine what percentage it represents of the entire time you spent on territory, you'll be amazed. It will certainly do much to help you adjust your attitude towards people who have little respect for your time, and you'll be itching for the challenge to do something about it at every single instance.

THE "TOO BUSY" BUYER

Good prospects are usually busy people, and the busier they are the more they're apt to buy—because their own business is obviously flourishing. Yet this becomes a problem to salespeople, particularly when the prospect makes the deadly statement, "I'm too busy to see you." It need not be so deadly. Never accept that statement as final. It rarely is. Instead, say, "I can understand how you feel. However, it will only take a

*For booklets and other materials produced by The Lacy Institute, write to: Mail Order Department, The Lacy Institute, 200 Clarendon Street, John Hancock Tower, Boston, Massachusetts 02116.

few minutes to show you how substantially you can increase your profits. Would another day be better for us to get together, say Tuesday or Thursday?" If the prospect says, "Yes, Thursday would be better," get an appointment and leave. When you come back on Thursday *you have an appointment*. And you know how sweet that is. We already discussed how to proceed under such circumstances.

Many times, however, a prospect will claim: "Every day is bad. I'm always busy. I just don't have the time." At this point you can say, "To work as hard as you do requires good nourishment, and I know just where we can have an excellent luncheon together and also talk." This may bring a smile, a lunch date, and an opportunity to do some selling. But should your prospect say, "I don't go out to lunch. I always eat in," suggest that you "brown bag" it together. Ask what kind of sandwich you should bring for him, and what beverage he prefers. Now this may sound rather persistent to you. But let me tell you what usually happens. Your persistence is noticed and respected. A busy and successful business executive will look at you, smile, and think, Wouldn't it be great if our own salespeople were this aggressive. You will be surprised at how many times the "brown bag" strategy will work for you. I have done it myself and know well the rewards. I have "brown bagged" it with vice presidents and company presidents who were pressed for time, and you simply can't imagine what a friendly experience it is. Just picture two people sitting at the prospect's desk eating sandwiches together. No one interrupts, no phone calls are taken, and a warm rapport develops. The idea is to get enough time to make a presentation, however brief. To get that time may require the skillful application of strategy. You simply can't afford to let a prospect slip through your fingers just because there isn't enough time to see you. Of course, you could argue that great presentations aren't made with a mouth full while eating a sandwich with a prospect. You are right. It won't be the best presentation in the world. But I'll take that instead of no presentation at all. Wouldn't you?

Bear in mind that far too many prospects will go out of their way to impress you with how busy a schedule they have. Some will even take five or ten minutes to explain to you their schedule of appointments or the itinerary that they must follow. You almost feel like saying, "In the time you have taken to explain how busy you are, I could have made my presentation." But, obviously, you don't. Instead, you act suitably impressed at the importance of this individual, while at the same time never ceasing in your quest for the time to make your presentation.

DOING BUSINESS IN A RESTAURANT

Obviously there will be many buyers who will accept your invitation for lunch, or even for dinner. But you must be very careful, especially when these acceptances come altogether too quickly. You see, there are many buyers who never turn down an invitation. Certain prospects will accept your generosity knowing full well that giving you an order is something that will never come about. For such people, turning down the offer of free drinks and a free meal would represent a departure from their normal behavior. They are usually known as "freeloaders." They are always too busy to see you during business hours. But suggest lunch or dinner and they leap at the opportunity.

First of all, you must learn to recognize a freeloader when you become involved with one. Not only will these types accept every invitation you extend, but they will go so far as to invite themselves to have lunch with you at your expense. Furthermore, you will find that they will casually inquire as to where you are taking them, just to make sure that it's to a restaurant where liquor is served. To the average freeloader, the drinks are more important than the food. Secondly, you must become an expert at evaluating the progress you are making, from a business standpoint, with each person who

puts a dent in your expense account. After two bouts at a restaurant something of value should have developed for you, especially since the *second* meal will have been your *third*
meeting. You see, between meals you strategically work in another interview by calling on prospects in the mid-morning or
mid-afternoon, within two weeks of the previous meal. (Their
consciences will make them see you, even though they may be
busy.) If the account is big enough and the potential fantastic,
three meals (representing five interviews) is as far as you need
go without becoming a benefactor. And, naturally, you must
always ask for the order. "Breaking bread" together is a warm
and pleasant way to socialize, but don't lose sight of your mis-
sion. You are not a goodwill ambassador. Never forget that
you are there to sell something, and you won't sell without
asking for the order.

Freeloaders aside, there are specific strategies that you'll
need to use when you do take someone out to lunch or dinner
for genuine business purposes. Naturally, you must be in control at all times. And why not? You are the host, or hostess,
and you are paying the check. Therefore you control how
much your guest will drink, how much business talk will take
place, and when. You are a leader and you are going to be in
charge of the situation.

Always arrange to arrive at a restaurant before the place
gets crowded. By doing so you can usually get a booth in a
corner or secluded area where distractions will be minimal.
The next strategic task for you to accomplish is to control the
prospect's drinking. You'll find that most prospects will drink
cocktails—usually martinis straight up (no ice), because they
don't want the drinks to get diluted. Notice we said *drinks*. It
will be a rare day when prospects stop at just one. Most will
have two and some will even go to three, if you let them. But
let's get one thing straight. Three martinis before lunch bor-
ders on alcoholism. Most prospects will have eaten breakfast
in the vicinity of seven a.m. You will probably have lunch at
about twelve-thirty or one. Their stomachs will be empty as
can be, no food having been taken for five or six hours. Under

these circumstances, there is no way that three cocktails can be consumed without severely dulling the senses. The alcohol is absorbed very quickly. And how can you do business with someone in that condition?

Here is how you control a prospect's intake of alcohol—as well as your own. When the waiter or waitress asks if there will be cocktails, let your prospect order first (most prospects will do so almost automatically). Then order a *tall* drink for yourself. Whatever you drink—scotch, bourbon, or rye—have it with water or soda, in a tall glass. Once the drinks arrive, be sure to sip on yours slowly. In the time that it takes most prospects to down their first cocktail, you will only be half through your drink. When the waiter or waitress returns to ask if you'd like another round, *you* speak up and say that you are still working on yours but that your guest may like another. The prospect will feel a little guilty (very little) that you're not having another, but will say yes. At this point you tell your host or hostess that you will be ready to order when the drink arrives. Thus, in a subtle way, you have announced the cut-off point of this alcoholic spree: two cocktails for your prospect and one tall, watered-down drink for you. In this way you have tactfully avoided having to do business with an inebriated prospect, while keeping yourself completely sober and sharp. You have also subtly directed the prospect to look at the menu and to be ready with a decision when the time comes to order. Try steering your prospect into ordering one of the "specials of the day." These are usually already prepared, lessening the possibility of "another round while waiting." You do this by saying something like, "The London broil sounds good." It may not be your prospect's choice but one of the other specials might be, now that you've brought the list of special meals to your prospect's attention.

Let us now address ourselves to the question of when is the best time to discuss business: before, during, or after the meal. The answer is obvious, yet most people who sell forget to use common sense. The best time is when you can make an abbreviated presentation without interruption. Certainly that can never happen during the course of the meal, when you can expect at least twelve interruptions. Think about it. Once you are seated with menus in hand, isn't this what generally happens?

> Waiter (or waitress) arrives to ask for drink order. (Interruption #1)
> Waiter delivers drinks. (Interruption #2)
> Waiter asks, "Another round?" (Interruption #3)
> Waiter delivers drink and takes order. (Interruption #4)
> Waiter serves food. (Interruption #5)
> Waiter asks if everything is satisfactory. (Interruption #6)
> Waiter clears plates and takes dessert order. (Interruption #7)
> Waiter serves dessert and coffee. (Interruption #8)
> Waiter offers more coffee. (Interruption #9)
> Waiter brings check. (Interruption #10)
> Waiter picks up check (with cash or credit card). (Interruption #11)
> Waiter brings change or sales slip to be signed. (Interruption #12)

If you were making a presentation in an office or home and there were twelve interruptions, how effective would you be? Then how can you hope to conduct any amount of business in a restaurant with at least twelve interruptions automatically scheduled to take place?

Here is some sensible strategy. Spend the major portion of the time at the restaurant *socializing*. Ask your prospects about hobbies, family, and so forth. Let them talk about themselves without limitation. Allow them to indulge in discussing their most favorite subject, themselves. Then, as the dessert order is being taken, ask for a pot of coffee and the check. Settle the latter as soon as it is presented. Then take complete control of the conversation to discuss the business you had in mind. You will accomplish much more in ten or fifteen minutes of uninterrupted conversation at the end of the meal than at any other time. Besides, those two cocktails your prospect has consumed will have been substantially absorbed by the food, and you will be working on a clear mind that can be sold.

A substantial amount of business is done daily over lunch or dinner, but all too often a great deal of money spent on food and drink is literally wasted. Like anything else connected with selling, the taking of a prospect or client to a restaurant should be done properly and not without advanced planning. It is a way of doing business under more pleasant circumstances and in better surroundings than are found in a place of business. You have merely shifted the locale. Don't ever forget that. Your prospects know why you are entertaining them, so they won't fault you or get restless when you bring up business before leaving the restaurant.

OVERLOOKED STRATEGIES

There are at least five strategies—personal-type strategies—that salespeople should be aware of at all times. They spell the difference between an average salesperson and a professional one, and should be practiced in every selling situation.

Remove your coat.   When the weather makes it necessary for you to wear a raincoat, topcoat, or overcoat, there is always the tendency to leave it on throughout the day. I've heard salespeople say, "I will make ten to fifteen calls a day. Do you expect me to take my coat off and put it on again fifteen times?" The answer is yes. Never be involved in a selling situation while wearing a coat. Psychologically it is working against you. While you are making your presentation the prospect is thinking of how warm you must be with your coat on; that perhaps you're not going to stay that long, since you didn't remove your coat; or that your raincoat is wet and you are ruining that newly upholstered chair. Do you see what is happening? Your coat is becoming the focus of attention, rather than your presentation. Besides, as a professional salesperson and a leader, you should be stripped for *action*. That means no coat on, and certainly no rubbers or boots. When you're selling, you're on center stage and you should be dressed accordingly—ready to make things happen. Make it a practice to leave the coat in the reception area. Don't even bring it in with you over your arm. When you enter the selling arena, you must be completely ready for business and free of all impediments.

Coffee? Politely decline.   How warm and friendly it is when the prospect greets you with, "Would you like to have a cup of coffee?" Most salespeople will jump at this marvelous opportunity to socialize while doing business. Right? *Wrong.* You must always refuse this kind gesture with a pleasant, "No, thank you, I've already had some." And here's the reason: you are there to do business and you want every minute to count. You want no interruptions of any kind and you want constant eye contact with your prospect. Look at what happens when you accept a cup of coffee. First the secretary has to ask you how you take it. Do you take it black, with one or two sugars, with cream? Sometimes a discussion may ensue as to whether you would like a donut or a sweet roll. Then the secretary returns with your coffee, looks for a coaster, carefully places it on the edge of your prospect's desk, and leaves. By now you have wasted valuable selling time, and were probably interrupted at a most important point in your presentation when your coffee was brought in. But there's more. From that point on, every time you reach for the cup to take a sip, you will break eye contact with the prospect. You will look at your cup and so will your prospect—every time you pick it up or set it down. Does this really make sense? Is a cup of coffee that important to you? To make matters worse, the prospect might begin to wonder if your cup isn't too close to the edge of the desk, fearing that it might topple over. And imagine what would happen to your entire presentation if, while presenting samples or literature to the prospect, you did happen to knock the cup over, spilling the coffee all over the desk, onto the rug—or both. Now you can see what a handicap a simple cup of coffee can be to your selling activities.

Don't smoke.   Hopefully you are a nonsmoker (everyone knows that smoking is injurious to one's health). Let's assume, however, that you do smoke but are in the process of cutting down and eventually quitting. What do you do when the prospect offers you a cigarette? The best strategy is to say, "No, thank you." Even if your tongue is hanging out for one, summon the will power to turn it down. The reason? Much like the coffee, it is an eye contact breaker. You are on your way to making your presentation. You are doing a good job of it. But if you are smoking a cigarette, you'll have to set it down in the ashtray whenever you're handling samples or literature. And you'll have to flick the ashes. Of course, every time you flick the ashes your eyes go to the ashtray, and so do your prospect's. It is bad enough that this will happen while your prospect smokes. By not smoking yourself, you at least cut down the number of times eye contact is broken by fifty percent. Moreover, isn't there the possibility that in your excitement over your presentation you may forget to flick the ashes into the ashtray, causing them to fall onto the rug? Isn't it also possible that in the shuffling of papers your cigarette could be knocked out of the ashtray and onto the desk top? Or on the rug? Do you need these possible problems during a presentation? Is that what you went there for, so that you and the prospect could both stare at ashtrays? Nonsensical, isn't it?

Close the distance.   In many instances you may end up sitting too far away from the prospect. The office may be large and the chair that was offered you a substantial distance from that of the prospect's. Under such circumstances, whenever possible, you should close the distance between yourself and the prospect. You do this strategically. As soon as you have reached a point in your presentation where you're about to show your product, explain something in your literature, or go over drawings, you rise from your chair and bring the materials to the prospect. Then you bring your chair in closer, closing up the gap. Now you are sitting a lot closer to the prospect than when you started. As a result, you create a better rapport, more warmth, and greater opportunity to point to things in your literature that you want your prospect to see. Suffice it to say that it is usually much easier to sell someone at close range than it is from across the room—psychologically speaking.

Use first names. By all means, whenever possible, you should make an attempt to get on a first name basis with your prospects and customers. This doesn't mean that you should be overly familiar. That would be a mistake and could bring about a deterioration in business relationships. But when done right, the first name strategy will prove most helpful by putting you and the prospect on the same plane. This is especially important when your object is to convince prospects that you can do as much for them by selling to them as they can do for you by buying. You must not jump into this situation, however, unless you know that you are on firm ground. First of all, try to determine whether or not the customer *wants* to conduct business on a first name basis. This is easier to find out on the telephone than in person. When a prospect answers the phone with, "Ms. Smith here," you know that she wants to be called Ms. Smith. On the other hand, if she opens with, "This is Jane Smith," she has already told you that she prefers to be called Jane. In person, though, it is not quite so easy. Let's assume you are calling on Mr. Jones. The secretary gives you permission to enter his office. You walk in and make your approach. Mr. Jones doesn't have to introduce himself, however. Under these circumstances you must assume that he wants to be called Mr. Jones. And you call him that whenever you are able to interject his name into the presentation. Soon, however, you will be able to evaluate his personality. After all, you are going to let him do some of the talking. Depending on how he acts and what he says, you will get a good fix on his personality. If you decide that he is the type that can be classified as rigid, cold, or extremely formal, then you know that your best bet is to continually call him Mr. Jones. On the other hand, if his personality is outgoing, down to earth, rather warm, and friendly, you may take the liberty of using the strategy that works more often than not. Assuming that you have been able to maneuver your chair next to his and assuming that the interview is going well from your standpoint, take the following action: right in the middle of one of your convincing statements, when you're bubbling with warmth as well as enthusiasm, look him in the eye, place your hand on his arm, and say, "It's all right to call you Fred, isn't it?" Ninety-nine times out of a hundred he's going to say, "Of course it is." But remember: this must be done at the opportune time, with a genuine smile, and when your instinct tells you that it's okay to pull it off.

HANDLING EGOTISTS

You will agree that one of the most difficult prospects to handle is the egotist. These individuals find it very hard to get their minds off of themselves long enough to give consideration to the proposition of a salesperson.

There are two kinds of egotists. The first consists of people who have little or nothing on the ball. Yet, to hear them tell it, you would think that they're God's gift to the universe. They will tell you how good they are, how important they are in the company, and how much better they do their jobs than anyone else that they know. Some even go so far as to explain all of the diplomas and awards on their office walls. This may sound far-fetched, but you have probably run into such people and will continue to run into them again and again.

There is not very much that you can do with prospects like these other than to be as humble as you possibly can (that's what they want) and try very hard to find some quality for which you can express your honest appreciation. They will elaborate on your comment at length and as they do so, you must find a way to turn their attention to your proposition and keep it there. If you are successful, you may be able to get through to them. But it's not easy. Such prospects are very hard to sell because of the patience and perseverance required on your part. The time involved may very well not be worth your while. Only you can decide this. Fortunately, not too many individuals in important business positions fall into this category. Usually egotists of this kind are not at all as important as they claim to be. Therefore, always consider the possibility that you are dealing with the wrong person. You see, this individual may not even be a decision maker. (If it's any consolation, you will find that whenever you encounter an egotist of this type you can be practically certain that six months from that date, upon your return, this person will no longer be there. Such egotism always catches up with people.)

The second type of egotist is the prospect who is good and knows it. At least here you have something to work with. Usually this is a self-made, successful individual. More often than not, you are dealing with a person in middle management who is ready to move into top management, a vice president, or a president of a company. These people usually have a tremendous respect for their own time. Not only are they difficult to see, but when you do get the opportunity you are usually given a quick, stand-up interview. Now, you know very well that you cannot make a decent sales presentation when you are given one or two minutes in a stand-up situation. It just doesn't pay. There is a definite strategy you can use, however. You apply what is known as reverse salesmanship. You make a challenging statement, something like, "I don't see how you can use my proposition to your advantage." This actually challenges them to prove to you that they *can* use it. The proposition of conquering obstacles or accomplishing the seemingly impossible represents a challenge that few people of this type can resist. Invariably they will set out to prove that they *can* do the exceptional thing. See what you did? You hit a central nerve, a dominant Hot Button. Successful, self-made individuals thrive on challenges. They almost go around looking for them. Why? Because that's what made them so successful. To them, everything is a challenge. And when you tell them that you don't think that they can utilize the benefits of your product or service, the challenge is clear. They make the sale for you. One word of warning is in order here. While it is true that reverse salesmanship will work most of the time, it should only be used when you have determined that your prospect falls into the category just described. Under any other circumstances re-·verse salesmanship can backfire on you, and usually does. When this happens you have automatically, and in very short order, lost the sale. In fact, you will have lost the sale even before you make your presentation. The wrong individual, having been thrown the challenge, will look at you and say, "That's right, we can't use what you're selling." Where do you go from there, except out?

SOCRATIC SALESMANSHIP

There are many styles of salesmanship. I am sure that you have heard many salespeople say that they have developed their own style, or have adopted the style of someone whom they admire. But without question, the most strategic style of all is that which is known as **Socratic salesmanship**. This type of selling is named after the man who perfected it—Socrates. He was a Greek philosopher and sage born almost 500 years before Christ. He developed a philosophy of salesmanship that has held up through the ages. It is still in use today by many of the best producers in all lines of selling.

The Socratic method consists of questions by which the prospect's thinking is guided to the only correct conclusion possible: the ultimate truth. When Socrates did the selling, the prospect did most of the talking while the philosopher sat back and figured out the reaction as well as the next question to fire back. He became so good at this that he rarely missed a sale.

One of the most strategic and effective things that you can do is to train yourself in the Socratic method of salesmanship. Ask questions, but make sure they are leading questions which guide the interview in the direction of a single, ultimate conclusion: a service for the prospect and a sale for you. When you sell this way, you benefit from at least five important advantages:

1. You pay your prospects a tremendous compliment by giving them a chance to talk about their problems, aims, opinions, and ideas. You endear yourself to every prospect because everyone loves a good listener.

2. You get an opportunity to think and size up the situation. You will be able to figure out the chief ambitions of your prospects, how you can help them to accomplish them, what type of mind they have, and what advantages will most appeal to them. This will help you to intelligently select the next question you will use in order to bring the presentation closer to your objective.

3. You learn from everyone. People in positions of any importance in business today have something on the ball, and by listening you are constantly learning and acquiring knowledge which will help you in other sales situations.

4. You will stay out of arguments. It is virtually impossible for you to get into an argument unless you express an opinion. And it is nearly impossible to express an opinion if you stick to the questioning method.

5. You cannot ask intelligent questions of anyone unless you think about their problems and ambitions. When you concentrate on thinking about your prospect's situation, you are automatically prevented from thinking about yourself. If you don't think about yourself, you won't talk about yourself. And once you reach that stage you will transform the world in which you live, for the better.

With so many benefits to be derived from the use of Socratic salesmanship, you would do well to adopt this style almost immediately. Many salespeople pay lip service to the statement,

"Always let the prospect talk." But give a salesperson the opportunity to make a presentation and you will find that the
prospect hardly has a chance to get a word in edgewise. The
Socratic method makes this type of prospect treatment
impossible.

THE PROSPECT WHO WON'T TALK

How do you handle the kind of prospect who won't talk—the
individual who sits and looks at you and says absolutely nothing throughout the entire interview? Prospects of this type
may be looking directly at you, but you know full well that
their minds are far from the room in which you are in. Then
there are those who won't even look at you while you are making your presentation. They will give regular glances at the
correspondence on the desk, or even stare out the window to
see what the weather is doing.

The best way to sell prospects like these is to ask a direct
question, then look at them and wait for the answer. You must
remember not to speak again until they answer, no matter
what happens. It's a sort of game: the person who speaks first
loses. Of course, your speechless prospects will be slightly em-
barassed. They'll probably ask you to repeat the question (con-
firming that no attention was being paid to you). And then
they'll answer it. But one thing is certain. From that moment
on, the prospect will be listening for the rest of the interview.
It's a little hard to do this to people, but it must be done. Any
presentation you make that falls on deaf ears is a complete
waste of your time. You simply cannot afford that.

NEW PRODUCT OR SERVICE
STRATEGY

Whenever the opportunity presents itself, use some strategy in
connection with new developments in your line. Before an-

nouncing a new product or service, a new model, or a new proposition, ask your prospects and customers what they think of it. It may sometimes be too late to incorporate their ideas, but you'll be surprised at how impressed they are that you considered their opinions. When you come back later to sell them the new developments, you'll get a most positive reaction. They will almost feel as though they have an owner's stake in it. You will enjoy the pleasant sales climate that develops as a result of this particular strategy.

SOCIAL SALESMANSHIP

Many businesses entail the use of **social salesmanship**—that is, entertainment on the golf course, at the baseball game, at the seashore, or over the weekend. Naturally, each occasion presents its own specific circumstances. Your judgment will tell you how to handle yourself. As a general rule, however, it is strategic in such circumstances to say absolutely nothing about the business you are seeking unless your host or guest initiates the discussion. It is much more important to concentrate on socializing and discussing the matters your prospects prefer to talk about. Your prospects are fully aware of your desire to obtain their business. They will admire and have more respect for you if you don't bluntly capitalize on any social advantage you may have for the moment. Should they initiate the discussion, then this changes matters materially and permits you to discuss a little business. Even then, however, you should leave the closing of actual sales for the office. If your prospects don't bring up business, then leave it undiscussed. Just before parting, let them know how much you enjoyed the occasion, and tell them that you plan to drop in and see them at their office in the near future. Remember how we said that people will go out of their way to do business with people they like? Well, using discretion when socializing with prospects is a golden opportunity to get them to like you.

On the subject of discretion, we too often forget what this word means. Here are three don'ts which will help define the limits of discreet behavior:

1. **Don't** play golf or any other sport or game for high stakes. If you happen to win a large sum of money from any prospect or customer, you'll leave a bad taste in their mouths. Why do it? They won't like you for it. In fact, they will never forget it. It will come up over and over again in conversations in the future.

2. **Don't** become a drinking partner to any of your customers. They may tell you how much they enjoy going out with you to "tie one on," but beware the next morning when they will have easily forgotten how silly *they* acted, while vividly remembering *you* in the condition *you* were in. That picture in the mind of your customers will never help your image.

3. **Don't** ever set up a social date for a prospect or customer. Even when asked to do so, you must graciously bow out by saying that you simply do not know anyone. After all, you are not in that business. Stay away from it; it can do you more harm than good. You are a salesperson, not a matchmaker.

ON REMEMBERING NAMES

It is a distinct advantage in sales work to remember names. Remembering faces is never enough. People like you to know their names. You will agree that when you have just met someone who continues to refer to you by name throughout that very first conversation, you find it very pleasing and decide that you like this person. You feel that he or she has an interest in you and wants to remember your name, as opposed to the joker who knows you fairly well but can never remember it and fakes it by greeting you with, "Hi, Handsome," or "Hi, Tiger."

The strategy of remembering names is not difficult to master. It's just a case of following four simple rules every time you meet someone for the first time:

1. *Understand the name correctly.* Many people don't pronounce their names clearly. Some have complicated or unusual ones. It is essential that you understand a name and how it is spelled if you are to remember it. If you don't catch it the first time you hear it, ask the person to repeat it for you. This genuine interest will never offend people. They will not only be happy to repeat their names for you, but they'll even spell them voluntarily if their name is an unusual one.

2. *Say it three times.* In your conversation with a new acquaintance, make sure that you say his or her name at least three times. Work it into every second or third sentence. By doing so you implant this new name in your own mind while, at the same time, pleasing the individual you've just met. You will never meet a person who doesn't like the sound of his or her name.

3. *Associate.* As you chat with new people, imagine their names written across their foreheads and try to associate them with some other person or idea. If they resemble a certain actress or actor, for example, make a mental note of this fact. Such associations will help you considerably. (I can recall having trouble remembering the name of a man who lived at the end of our street. Yet Jack Hennessey is certainly an easy name. Then I made an association: from that day on, whenever I saw him, I would think of cognac and Hennessey would pop instantly up in my mind.)

4. *Write it down.* As soon as possible after you've left a new acquaintance, write that person's name down in your notebook, your records, or wherever you keep items you want to remember. Seeing it on paper helps you even more. In addition, jot down any association you were able to make. Seeing this on paper burns it into your brain more deeply.

Bring these four simple rules into play from now on and you will be amazed at your increased ability to remember names. You won't have to place yourself in the embarassing position of having to make the age-old statement, "Gee, I remember your face but I simply can't recall your name." That's not only a rusty phrase, but one that hurts the other person's pride. All individuals on the face of this earth like to think that they are unusual enough for you to easily remember their names whenever you see them.

The various strategies discussed in this chapter will all prove helpful to you over and over again. But they will never represent substitutes for hard work and mastery of your proposition, two foundations which are vital. Add some of these strategies, however, and you will augment your selling power substantially. There will be many times, on the other hand, when you have done an excellent selling job and have used the best strategies that applied, but didn't allow for the unexpected. And the unexpected happens more than we like to realize. This is clearly demonstrated in the story about two salesmen who had been roommates in college. After not seeing each other for fifteen years, they meet one day and begin bringing each other up to date. One tells how he's married, has three kids, owns a nice home in the suburbs, and has two cars. Everything's fine. Then he says, "But enough about me. How about you?"

"Well," his friend confides, "I'm not even married."

"What? A handsome guy like you?"

"Well, it isn't because I haven't tried. I live with my parents, and every time I get serious about a girl I bring her home and my mother turns her down. But last week I used some salesmanship. I brought home a girl that looks like my mother, acts like her, talks like her, has the same personality— clearly a younger carbon copy."

"Great! So what happened?"

"No deal. My Dad couldn't stand her!"

One never knows just what will work. But you must do all in your power to be fully prepared for every single sales call.

You must also be prepared for the unexpected—or at least as prepared as possible. Learn as many sales strategies as you can and always have them ready to put to use. Most of the time, you'll be able to dig yourself out of almost any situation. But I repeat: there will be unexpected occurrences. Every so often a prospect will do or say something that you least expected. You must never let this shock you. Learn to remain calm, cool, and collected under any and all circumstances. Once you learn to control your emotions to that degree, you can then rest assured that no prospect will ever see you with your jaw locked—in the yawn position.

SALES STRATEGIES CHECKLIST

	Always	Some-times	Never
As soon as I have waited ten to fifteen minutes to see a prospect, I take proper action.	☐	☐	☐
The "too busy" response stirs me into aggressively seeking a luncheon or "eat-in" situation.	☐	☐	☐
I recognize and properly handle "freeloaders."	☐	☐	☐
I control any drinking when dining with a prospect.	☐	☐	☐
I avoid making a presentation over lunch until the meal is over and no further interruptions are expected.	☐	☐	☐
I remove my coat before making a sales presentation.	☐	☐	☐
Politely, I turn down coffee offers made by prospects.	☐	☐	☐
I refrain from smoking during a presentation.	☐	☐	☐
I attempt to get on a first name basis with prospects and customers.	☐	☐	☐

I am able to properly
handle egotists.

My presentation utilizes
the Socratic style of
salesmanship.

I avoid discussing busi-
ness when socializing
with prospects or cus-
tomers.

I have trouble remem-
bering people's names.

Note: See Appendix section for correct answers.

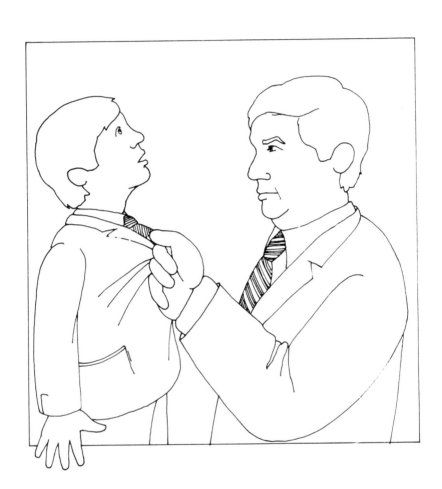

eight

POWER THROUGH ASSERTIVENESS

By this time most of us are aware that selling and leadership go hand in hand. We know that a leader is always able to exercise control. And we know that a salesperson is always in control during the selling process.

Control and power also go hand in hand. After all, if you have control over a situation, this is power. And in this chapter we will explore how a great deal of power is generated through assertiveness.

WHAT IS ASSERTIVENESS?

In the recent past, much has been written and said on the subject of assertiveness. A great deal of it paints a highly sophisticated, psychological picture that the average salesperson would run away from. Assertiveness need not be so complex—and it isn't.

135

First of all, let's define the meaning of assertion.

Assert: to join to; to claim; to state positively, declare, or affirm; to maintain or defend (rights, claims, etc.).

Assert oneself: to insist on one's rights, or on being recognized; to speak with implicit confidence in the truth of one's statement, from one's knowledge of the matter.

As you can clearly see, these definitions have nothing to do with selling. They are very general. They apply to people of all types. And that's just the point. Assertiveness (like salesmanship) isn't something you turn on when needed and turn off when not required. It has to be part of your makeup—all the time. Perhaps you don't consider yourself to be an assertive individual. "I never have been," you might say, "and I doubt that I can change that." Fear not. You definitely can—and you will.

To begin with, take stock of your present position on this subject. How often do you:

- get what you want or need
- get the opportunity to express your feelings
- get to tell your whole story without being cut off
- get to achieve your goals and achieve them on schedule

Well, how did you fare? If you couldn't truthfully say, "almost always" to all four, you need to work on your assertiveness skills. But you mustn't feel badly. Most people require such training but do nothing about it. You are different—you are going to take action.

First of all, decide that you will pay close attention to the content of your daily verbal communication with others (this means *everyone*). Is it positive and effective, or do you sometimes come across as a wishy-washy personality? Check to see if you have been using any of the phrases in the list that follows. They reflect nonassertive behavior and they all serve to diffuse meaning and avoid directness.

Statement	*Effect*
I think so, too	avoids participation in a discussion
I kinda think	conveys inability to express exactly what you think
I guess I want	conveys inability to express exactly what you want
Gee, I really don't know	conveys vast indecision
I could never do that	conveys lack of confidence, "poor me"
I'm sorry, but	expresses an apology followed by justification
Did I do all right?	expresses insecurity
It's not my fault	blames others to slip out of a situation
Don't you see the humor in it?	makes a joke out of a serious situation
Here's how I decided	conveys the need to rationalize decisions
You better listen, or	threatens people to make them listen

From now on, listen carefully to what you say. Better still, if you have a file of letters and memoranda you have written, dig it out and read over some of your written communications. As you do, underline phrases that reflect indecision, insecurity, or lack of clear thinking—anything that's indirect or that tends to diffuse your meaning as exemplified by the phrases previously listed. Some of these may be pet phrases that are a standard part of your everyday vocabulary. I suggest that you jot them down on a separate sheet of paper, then look them over regularly in training yourself to avoid them.

I shall never forget an incident in my life that relates perfectly to this very point. I had been recalled to active duty by the Navy during the Korean conflict, sent to Davisville, Rhode Island, and appointed Industrial Relations Officer for the base. As such, I was responsible for personnel administration involving 2500 civilian employees. About a year later an RIF was ordered: a reduction in force of 500 workers. I had to administer it. Now, these were all Civil Service employees. So I couldn't simply pick out the people we could manage without (making sure that the drones were included) and let them go. Oh, no. We had to follow Civil Service procedures whereby people with seniority—with certain skills, and at certain levels— would "bump" others, who would be terminated instead. When we had completed this monsterous reshuffling of people on paper and had developed the list of those to be terminated, one more step remained. An official from the 1st Naval District had to be summoned to review the entire RIF. We sent for him and he came.

Now, to me, this whole matter was extremely important. We were dealing with people's lives, their means of support for themselves and their families. Some would have to move out of the area because they possessed specialized skills that only a Naval base could utilize. Each decision had to be justified on paper, and I proceeded to ask this official if our thinking on each one had been correct. His answer? "I would suspect so." After a whole day and several hundred 'I would suspect sos' I was ready to climb the wall. When he left, I called in my four department heads, expressed my concern, and convinced them that we should rematch all of the decisions with the RIF regulations. After two eighteen-hour days, we were satisfied that this responsibility had been properly handled. But we found that three changes had to be made. Three people, originally scheduled for termination, would now remain while three others would be terminated in their place. So I phoned our nonassertive official, explained the three changes, and asked him if he agreed with our thinking and would reapprove the RIF. His answer? "I would suspect so."

Offensively Aggressive Behavior

We must get one thing straight. Assertiveness does not mean being unpleasant, deliberately offensive, or abrasive in any way. You can be clear, direct, decisive, and confident without being disagreeable. Certainly, in selling, you won't survive if you are disagreeable to any degree. A prospect or customer simply doesn't have to put up with you. If your competitor is more pleasant, that's where the orders will go.

Yet, whan many people make the decision to be more assertive, they begin to act superior to everyone around them in the process. They find it necessary to use "put down" words, make "loaded" comments, and project an almost hostile personality. They think that they have been successful by having put others on the defensive. And often this is done in a loud voice, with a cold stare, and with a domineering attitude.

It is one thing to be aggressive, in the assertive sense of the word, but quite another to be *offensively* aggressive. The latter has absolutely no place in selling. In fact, it should be avoided in life, regardless of the area of endeavor.

BOOSTING YOUR ASSERTIVENESS

Obviously, it is extremely difficult to pinpoint specific rules, in sequential order, for the development of assertiveness. The reason it's difficult is because, as we all know, no two people are exactly alike. One person may be somewhat assertive already, while another may be altogether too assertive. Your first step, then, is to evaluate the extent of your own assertiveness. Then you can make the necessary adjustments.

Generally speaking, however, there *are* some ground rules that can be followed and which should be kept in mind on a regular basis. First of all, an assertive person sits and walks comfortably erect, with a confident facial expression. Without question, this applies to everyone. Then, giving special attention to your weak points, make an effort to follow these rules:

• Speak up firmly when unfair demands are made of you.
• Be able to complete a sentence without being interrupted by others.

- Speak clearly and firmly enough so that others understand what you want.

- Use a pleasant questioning technique (by asking who, what, where, how, when).

- Initiate cooperative efforts by making statements such as, "Let's work this out," or, "Let's think it out together."

- Get people to do things your way, cooperatively and without disdain.

- Speak in a clear, relaxed voice that projects sufficiently without overpowering people (review the diaphragmatic breathing exercises in Chapter 3).

You will agree that some of these rules apply directly to salespeople. For instance, sitting erectly while making a sales presentation is an absolute must. Yet, while supervising and working with them on territory, I found that any number of salespeople would make themselves quite at ease during a presentation, sliding down in their chairs, crossing their legs, and appearing as relaxed as one would be in a reclining chair at home. Such posture almost tells the prospect, "I don't really care whether you buy from me or not." You can rest assured that no salesperson under my supervision ever pulled this twice. In fact, at sales meetings I always pointed out that successful salespeople can always be spotted by physicians during a physical. The have an indentation midway on the underside of each thigh due to sitting erectly—on the edge of the chair.

Speaking clearly and with good projection is also essential. How could a salesperson hope to convince a prospect to buy if the prospect isn't catching half of what is being said. It's a mistake to assume that everyone has good hearing, especially prospects who are getting along in years (see the discussions of enunciation and projection in Chapter 3). In order for your presentation to sink in and sell, it must be heard and clearly understood. And you can only assert yourself with a voice that projects.

Examples of Assertiveness in Selling

The buying committee problem.   If you sell a product to large organizations, associations, or chain store operations, you have probably run into the problem of the **buying committee**. When a buying committee is involved, it means that the person on whom you make sales calls does not have complete authority to give you an order. The decision has to be made by the committee. You are allowed to make the presentation and to leave samples or literature. Then the buyer will tell you that all of this will be brought to the attention of the buying committee, and that you will be informed of the decision afterward. Now, you could be consoled because you were at least able to make the presentation, and because you do have someone who's going to follow through for you. But that would be the attitude of a nonassertive individual. What you should do under the circumstances is assert yourself by saying something like, "I greatly appreciate your willingness to bring my product to the attention of the buying committee, Mr. Jones. However, as you know, there are always questions that come up, and I will be very happy to attend the meeting and provide the answers. Now, Mr. Jones, when will the meeting be held?" About fifty percent of the time you will have gotten yourself on the agenda of the next meeting, and you will be able to make a presentation to those who *can* make a decision. The other fifty percent of your attempts will produce a no. The buyer will say something like, "Oh, we never allow outside salespeople to attend our buying committee meetings." Is this the end of your assertiveness? Not yet. You will follow up with, "I can understand the policy, Mr. Jones. However, do I have your assurance that my product will be brought up for consideration?" He says, "Yes," and you leave. Any more room for assertiveness? You bet. Now you write a letter timed to arrive prior to the meeting. In it, you thank Jones for the time he spent with you and for agreeing to bring up your product for consideration at the next buying committee meeting. Then you go on to state that you have attached a sheet listing all product benefits in order of their importance, to save him the time of having to glean them from the literature that you left behind. See what you've done? You have not rested comfortably with the fact that someone else is going to do your selling for you (it's never the same). And what do you think the buyer is going to do with the sheet of paper you've attached with the letter? You can be sure that he will bring it with him to the meeting because it makes his job a lot easier. This method of dealing with the buying committee, a perfect example of assertive aggressiveness, has worked over and over again throughout the years. If it fits into your scheme of things, start using it at once.

Dealing with purchasing agents.   If your product is used by OEM accounts (Original Equipment Manufacturers) you've probably run into the constant problem of having to do business with the purchasing agent alone. Under no circumstances are you allowed to set foot into the manufacturing area to talk to the production manager, the engineers, or the machinists. That's forbidden territory. Why? Because purchasing agents want complete authority, and because they want the option to shop around and get the best price. Of course, they must go along with specifications from department heads within their companies when asked or forced to do so, but such specifications are difficult to come by if you can't get into the shop and speak to those who are in a position to specify. Assertiveness, here, is the answer. You must get to certain people inside the company or your product will never be specified. So you send literature to the individuals involved, and then you phone them to ask if they received it. Naturally, in the course of the conversation, you are able to further extoll the benefits of your product. Then you maneuver the conversation towards an agreement that an in-person discussion would be most worthwhile in determining how the product meets the company's needs. And you make an appointment. When you go to make the sales call you won't be automatically funnelled into the purchasing agent's office, because you have an appointment with someone else. Let's face it, the purchasing agent won't like it too much. But there isn't very much any purchasing agent can do after the people you call on specify that they want your product. And that's what you set out to do, isn't it? Some salespeople will argue that such tactics are unfair to the purchasing agent. Well, it's unfair of the purchasing agent never to allow you to make a presentation to those people who understand what your product is all about. No purchasing agent understands everything about all products. Most of them operate like machines. A product is needed, they look up the manufacturer with the best price, they order it, and they consider their job done. But the best price doesn't always indicate the best product. We all know that.

I suppose assertiveness could be called a speaking up for your rights. Not boisterously or offensively, but firmly and pleasantly. It's absolutely amazing what happens when you continually assert yourself. The end result is usually a terrific feeling of accomplishment. To stay in condition, you should assert yourself for the little things as well as the big. Then your assertiveness will remain constant. I had occasion to practice this theory recently, when I received a letter from *Time Magazine* advising me that my subscription was about to expire and that I should renew. However, absolutely no mention was made of a huge, updated almanac which I had seen heavily advertised as a gift for new subscribers to the magazine. I couldn't help but feel that this was somewhat unfair. So I wrote a note to the director of marketing of that publication. I pleasantly explained that I did not think it was fair to make a gift of a beautiful almanac to a brand new subscriber and to deny people like myself, who have been buying and reading the magazine for years while never qualifying for a promotional premium. I signed it and felt good about having done my assertiveness exercise for the day. My communication was never answered. But within one week I received an almanac and a bill to cover my renewal.

HOW POWER IS DEVELOPED

All of us have heard it said that in selling it is important to have confidence and power in dealing with people. We discussed where confidence comes from in Chapter 2. Power, as you may have guessed, comes mostly from assertiveness. Every time that you assert yourself with success you not only feel good about it, but you also come closer to the realization that assertiveness gives you a lot more power than most people have.

It's really not that difficult to have more power than others. You see, the majority of people are followers. We know that. Somehow, though, we repeatedly fail to capitalize on it. Perhaps what we need is constant proof that most of the people around us are, indeed, followers. You can see this by observing other drivers the next time you're in your car. When you find yourself in a standing line of traffic at a stoplight, pull up about two feet closer to the car ahead of you. Then look in your rear view mirror. You'll see that the cars behind you have pulled up just as you did, even though the light is still red. Automatically they all followed the leader.

Once you become accustomed to leading people into doing things your way, your sales curve automatically takes a steep upward trend. But let's get more specific. When prospects are pressed for time they are apt to listen to your approach but leave you standing. Now, you know that a stand-up interview is never a satisfactory one. And it usually ends long before your presentation is complete. As an assertive individual, this is what you do. You look the prospect in the eye and say, pleasantly, "Let's sit down for a few minutes so I can show you how to reduce down time by 10%." You gesture towards a chair as you're saying this. You say nothing more. The prospect must take some action. More often than not your instructions will be followed.

Of course, there will be times when the prospect says, "I wish I could give you the time today but I'm just too busy to do so." Okay, no need to argue. You say, "I can understand how you feel, Mr. Jones. Why don't we set up this important meeting for another day?" Then you point to his calendar on the desk and you say, "Please check your calendar. Is next Tuesday a good day for you, or is Thursday better?" Now he looks at his calendar, decides on one day or the other and the time, and you walk out with an appointment. Your assertiveness has paid off again. You have exercised a tremendous amount of power over the prospect without antagonizing him in any way.

I'm sure you get the idea. The amount of power that can be achieved with assertiveness is simply unbelievable. It gives you the control you need to get things done your way. And it gives you the control necessary to close orders when indecision is working against you. You will recall how, in Chapter 5, we discussed the necessity of asking for the order a minimum of three and preferably five times. Most salespeople find it very difficult to ask for the order more than once or twice. Why? They are not assertive enough. The next time you're faced with an indecisive close, try taking the order pad out of your brief case, turning it to the proper page, inserting the carbon copy, and holding your pen ready in hand to write up the order. Look at the prospect with expectancy. And act suitably surprised if there's any hesitation. Expectancy develops even more power for you.

ASSUMED ASSERTIVENESS

Because most salespeople have above average egos, they assume that they are quite assertive. Usually they are assuming incorrectly. To become assertive and remain that way requires effort—ongoing effort—not only in selling situations, but in circumstances associated with everyday living as well. It requires being aware of when you've been "had," when and how you were "used," or how certain individuals "put one over on you." You allow these things to happen by not being assertive enough. It doesn't mean that others are more assertive than you are but that, for a variety of reasons, they have taken actions—or have failed to act—and you are victimized. But let's get more specific by referring to typical examples.

You have just made a purchase in a department store. The item has been wrapped and the sales slip is being written. But the phone rings, and the sales clerk gets into a long conversation with a prospective customer who's inquiring about the sizes and colors stocked of a particular item. All of this occurs while you wait for the completion of your transaction. Who is more important? You are there with money in hand. The caller could be at home, stretched out on a chaise lounge. Is this fair to you? Are you apt to interrupt the phone conversation and request that your transaction be completed?

Let's assume now that you are at your bank. You've been waiting in line to cash a check. Finally it's your turn, but as the teller begins to count out your money, a supervisor comes along and engages your teller in a lengthy conversation about a time card. You are pressed for time and you become increasingly annoyed. Do you boil inside and wait it out? Or are you apt to interrupt and say, "Pardon me, but may I have my money so I can go along?" Aren't you the *customer*?

Then, at the super market, you buy only about a dozen items. The check out clerk puts them all in one bag. Three items are sticking out over the top. It's a cinch that something will drop out as you go to your car. Will you condone the clerk's laziness and struggle with the overstuffed bag? Or will you assert yourself and insist that some of the items be put into another one?

Most likely you have experienced these very situations. If you did nothing about them, you were "had." But that's not as important as the fact that you didn't assert yourself. You see, your assertiveness level took a drop on each occasion. Let that happen enough times and you'll have no assertiveness at all. The result? Your sales curve will nose-dive proportionately. Much like the muscles in your body, your assertiveness needs constant exercising—not just when you're selling, but at any time when it's justifiable. Constant exercise of this kind will help keep you conditioned for survival in selling.

ASSERTIVENESS CHECKLIST

	Always	Some-times	Never
I'm able to make a presentation without being cut off.	☐	☐	☐
My verbal communication is positive.	☐	☐	☐
I speak up firmly when unfair demands are made of me.	☐	☐	☐
I'm able to get people to do things my way, cooperatively and without disdain.	☐	☐	☐
When making a presentation I sit up erectly.	☐	☐	☐
I exercise my assertiveness, even on little things, to stay in trim.	☐	☐	☐
I can exercise power over prospects without antagonizing them.	☐	☐	☐
I feel considerable power, gained from assertiveness, when asking for the order.	☐	☐	☐
I expect a prospect to say yes at the close.	☐	☐	☐
Certain people are able to take advantage of me.	☐	☐	☐

If something is impor-
tant I stand up for it.

When I decide that I
made a wrong purchase
at a "final" sale, I still
try to return it.

Note: See Appendix section for correct answers.

nine

COPING WITH STRESS

Those who survive and do well at selling have learned to cope with stress, knowingly or unknowingly. Some people naturally possess the type of personality that can handle just about any stressful situation with relative ease. If you fall into this category you are very fortunate, because most people don't. If while reading this you have already decided that you are one of these fortunate few, be careful: you may very well be wrong. Far too many people believe themselves most capable when it comes to coping with stress, and then wonder what happened when things went wrong in a tense situation. To compound the problem, they rationalize the result in a variety of ways, never once allowing the possibility that stress may have gotten the better of them.

In this chapter we will clearly explore what stress is all about and how it applies to salespeople. And we'll do this not only from a selling standpoint but from an everyday living perspective as well. Both are tied in with each other to a surprising degree.

RECOGNIZING STRESS

We all know what stress is. But do we recognize it for what it *really* is? Do we thoroughly understand its effect on us—both negatively and positively?

Stress is defined as the response of your body to any demand made upon it, whether that demand be real or imagined, pleasant or unpleasant. Dr. Hans Selye, acclaimed as the world's leading authority on stress, has said that, "One's positive mental attitude does influence personal outcome favorably and beneficial stress emerges from a constructive approach to life's calamities. To varying degrees we can thrive on stress."* Dr. Selye also claims, however, that stress-induced diseases are increasing in our society because a constantly changing environment makes near-impossible demands on the human mind and body. Stress can and does affect every aspect of life. He feels that while stress is necessary and unavoidable, too much of it produces staggering changes in intellectual and emotional attitudes, as well as in health.

Now that, in a nutshell, is what stress is all about. And I hasten to add that, in life there is stress *every single day*, some good, some bad. But every day of our lives we will encounter stress of some type. The real challenge lies in recognizing and coping with it.

A certain amount of stress in your lifetime is good. In fact, it is necessary, because stress is part of the body's program for survival in a rough, complicated world (and the world of selling can be particularly rough). Yet, too often, stress-producing activity is looked upon only in its negative form. Therefore we must first learn to recognize stress in both its harmful and valuable forms. We must hesitate long enough to categorize it, by asking ourselves, Is this stress situation **real** or **imagined**? And is it **pleasant** or **unpleasant**? If it's imagined and unpleasant, dismiss it from your mind at

*Dr. Hans Selye is founder and president of the International Institute of Stress and of the Hans Selye Foundation, Montreal, Quebec.

once. You are barking up the wrong tree and it's costing you. If it's real and unpleasant, apply the techniques of coping with it which we will discuss later in this chapter. If it's real or imagined, but pleasant, enjoy every second. Excitement from happiness, for instance, is a healthful kind of stress that you need not scrutinize. And a little pleasant daydreaming never proved too stressful to anyone.

General Stress Situations

In order to recognize and properly cope with negative stress, it is important to know the common sources from which it springs. At least six sources can be identified, and they affect people in varying degrees.

Work (Source 1).   One's work situation is considered the greatest source of injurious stress in our society today. Stress in the working world can arise from job dissatisfaction; fear of, or dislike for, one's supervisor; rivalry; lack of organization; lack of progress; unmeasurable productivity; boredom from repetition; and adherence to strict company policies.

Overcrowding (Source 2).   We all need space that we can call our own, be it mental or physical. Without it we become annoyed or even agitated. And this leads to stress. Some of the stressful situations we experience as a result of overcrowding include traffic jams; parking lots filled to capacity; clogged expressways; long lines accompanied by endless waiting; and the scarcity of vacancies or unavailability of reservations in airlines, restaurants, and hotels.

Time (Source 3).   In many instances your own procrastination or lack of organization will precipitate stressful situations. But there are also instances when they are brought about by the hectic pace of city living. Time-related stress can be triggered by racing with time; being regularly behind schedule; talkative prospects; slow and inept receptionists; traffic stop lights; long lines at toll booths; emergency car repairs; or difficult deadlines.

Finances (Source 4).   One of the most problematic sources of tension is an inflationary society. Stress is often most crippling and hardest to overcome when it is brought on by the inability to meet financial obligations. Some of the situations that provoke financially-related stress include insufficient income; unexpected expenses; no savings; unusually high debts; unmanageable household budgets; gambling losses; and the impulsive buying of unaffordable items.

Noise (Source 5).   You may have complained, on many occasions, that you could barely keep your thoughts straight because of continuous noise. Yet you probably didn't realize how much stress it was causing you. Noise can be blocked out, but only up to a point. Loud stereos, radios, and televisions, barking dogs, and screaming children are a few of the sounds that can occasion stress, as are slamming doors, horns and sirens, screeching tires, dripping faucets, power lawnmowers, and snowblowers.

Family (Source 6).   Living with one or more people and sharing things with them, including problems, can be a continual source of stress. Marriage, happy or not, will always produce a certain amount of stress. Some of the situations in which family-related stress is bound to arise include lack of mutual consideration; poor communications; arguments; lack of love and affection; jealousy; suspicion of infidelity; problems with children; or problems with relatives.

Be aware of all six of these sources, and be quick to recognize the stress produced. By learning to tune into your body and catch the signals of stress, you can cut down substantially on its injurious effects—both mental and physical.

THE EFFECTS OF STRESS

Our bodies are extremely sensitive. Normally we give this fact very little thought. But should our body temperature increase by one or more degrees, we're likely to feel terrible. Then we know that something is radically wrong. Yes, the sensitivity of the human body is amazing.

Equally amazing are the physical effects and behavioral changes that can be brought on by stress. Admittedly, people react to stress in a variety of ways. Some are able to cope more quickly and easily than others. And what one individual considers a very stressful situation, another may look upon as hardly stressful at all. Without question it's a personal matter. But when unpleasant stress is having an effect on a human being, there are definite and immediate physical signs. All or some of these will be experienced to some degree:

> increased heartbeat
> increased respiration
> elevated blood pressure
> increased perspiration
> increased blood flow to muscles
> muscle tenseness
> nervousness
> increased body metabolism

You will agree that all of these signs are most disturbing. Just think of the last time that you were actually awakened by a horrible nightmare. Your heart was pounding, you were covered with perspiration, and you were breathing heavily. Only when you fully realized that it was just a dream were you able to relax. Then, gradually, your body returned to normal. Incidentally, these imagined and unpleasant stress-producing situations are just as dangerous as the real ones. That's why, if you are the type who always imagines the worst, you are causing yourself undue stress that resolves nothing. If you carry these irrational thoughts in your mind for long periods of time you are headed for disaster because, after a steady diet of these "emergency responses," your body will remain permanently affected. Your blood pressure will stay up. Your organs will begin to fail. You will become defenseless against disease. In addition to the physical damage, you may also experience certain behavioral changes that will become noticeable to others, if not to yourself. And all of this because you produced so much stress within yourself—stress that may have been completely unwarranted.

The physical effects produced by excessive, unpleasant stress are many. Some are very serious. This partial list will have a sobering effect:

headaches	allergies	rapid heart rate
skin rashes	aching back and	excessive
stomach aches	limbs	sweating
hypertension	common colds	dizziness
muscle spasms	fatigue	asthma
indigestion	diarrhea	blurred vision
	vomiting	neck and shoulder tension

As for the behavioral changes mentioned earlier, here are just some of them:

nervous tics	frowning	hair twisting
teeth grinding	insomnia	nail biting
impatience	door slamming	tears
temper tantrums	changed	apathy
fist clenching	drinking, smoking, or eating habits	visible fear

Once you consider the physical effects and the behavioral changes caused by stress, you can begin to appreciate the tremendous importance of learning how to cope with stressful situations. From now on, at the very onset of a physical or emotional problem, you won't automatically dismiss the possibility that it was caused by stress. So many of us do just that and, in the process, fail to attack the cause for future avoidance.

STRESS IN SELLING

There are certain types of stress that salespeople regularly encounter. Each of these types can be traced to one of the six broad categories we've already discussed. It is important that we spotlight them here, however, so that you'll be sure to recognize them when they occur. Only then can you take the necessary steps to prevent adverse mental and physical effects.

First of all, there is the almost everyday stress of disappointment. You are disappointed when, after having made a professional and complete presentation, the prospect doesn't buy. Well, you should be disappointed—just enough to make you work a little harder on the next call—but not enough to cause injurious stress. Such stress will not only affect your health, but your pocket as well. You see, if you are still brooding over the sale you lost when you make your next presentation, it will show. Your face will reflect it and you won't be as enthusiastic. The result? Another turn down, adding even more stress.

It is certainly true that you must assume that you are going to sell each prospect at every sales call. In that frame of mind you make a better presentation. But it is also true that you will never reach the point when you'll sell every single prospect. Consequently, you must confront reality on a regular basis to avoid stress and survive. It is a smart salesperson who, after a gallant but failing effort, can walk away with a smile while internally saying, "Oh, well, you can't win them all."

Then there is the stress caused by certain prospects (or customers) who won't see you when you call. On occasion they will, but many times they'll insist that you make an appoint-

ment and return at a later time. You are not only disappointed, you are almost furious. After all, you have lost time in
attempting to make this sales call—and in selling, time is
money. But what can you do about it? You certainly can't
make people stop doing what is more important to them just
because you have arrived on the scene. And even if you could,
the reception you'd get would be far from favorable. There are
two ways through which to avoid stress from such situations:

1. Make a list of people who can rarely be seen without an
    appointment. Then, when preparing your itinerary, set up
    appointments with as many of them as possible. This will
    substantially decrease the number of times that this
    stressful situation will come up while on territory. And
    when you prepare your itinerary, send postal cards saying
    that you will be calling for an appointment. Then proceed
    to make these phone calls during working hours.
2. Develop the ability to place yourself in the other person's
    shoes. How would you like it, for example, if you were try-
    ing to do your work in an office where unexpected sales-
    people popped in constantly to interrupt you, taking up
    time you can ill afford to lose?

The first is a fairly obvious solution. But the second solution is
one that most of us accept, yet do little about. We are so concerned over our own aims and ambitions that we are quick to
forget that others have their aims and ambitions as well.

I learned a lesson about this very early in my sales career that I have never forgotten. It seems almost 100 years
ago that I was covering a Boston territory for a small phar-
maceutical manufacturer, using a Chevrolet that had seen its
best years. One morning I left my home in suburban Bel-
mont with the usual expectations of sales success, only to
discover, at the first major intersection, that I had no brakes.
At the nearest gas station I learned that the master cylinder
had to be replaced, so I left the car for the day. Taking my
detail bag, loaded with samples and literature, I walked to

the nearest bus stop. A ride to the Back Bay section of Boston would put me in an area where I could make many doctor calls in any one building.

Soon I was on my way, not in a bus, but in the back seat of a beautiful Cadillac. A surgeon on whom I regularly called was driving to Boston with his nurse, had recognized me, and had offered me a ride. How nice of him, I thought. But then, he was a very pleasant, easygoing, successful surgeon who had a nice way with people and took life in stride. It was not that surprising.

To bypass Harvard Square in Cambridge, the doctor took a side street. It was a narrow, one-way street with cars parked on either side, leaving room for only one lane of traffic. Near the end of that street we approached, and stopped behind, a car that had been left unattended. On the porch of a nearby house was the obvious driver, a Western Union messenger. (These were the days when a telegram would be delivered in the traditional, sealed yellow window envelope by a uniformed messenger in whose outstretched visored cap you would place a tip.) Now, this messenger had been ringing the doorbell to no avail. Yet he wouldn't give up. He kept ringing and ringing while the traffic backed up. The doctor's nurse, sitting up front, reached over and began to blow the majestic twin horns of the Cadillac in utter desperation. The blasts fell on deaf ears. The messenger kept ringing the door bell. And the doctor, smiling, turned to his nurse and said, "Marie, relax. If he knew any better, he wouldn't have that job." Marie allowed the incident to cause her considerable stress. The doctor, on the other hand, was able to put himself in the messenger's shoes and to accept the incident philosophically. It caused him no stress whatsoever.

Another type of stress related to selling is caused by setting unrealistic goals. The struggle to then attain them usually proves costly, due to the self-inflicted stress experienced in the process. Statements such as, "I'll double my sales this year," or, "I'll be promoted in less than two years," may sound very positive, aggressive, and entrepreneurial. But they may very well represent the beginning of the end. While it is important to have goals and to strive to attain them, make sure that you don't expect from yourself more than you can deliver.

If you are presently working as hard and as effectively as possible and your sales curve is rising at a rate that will produce a 30% increase over last year, how could you realistically expect a 100% increase? I realize that miracles do happen, but you will have to agree that they are rather scarce.

As far as being promoted is concerned, there are even more variables involved, over and above realism. Maybe you think that you are, or will be, the best salesperson in your district, and therefore the best candidate for promotion. The best candidate? By whose standards? Using whose guidelines? By now everyone knows that the person with the best sales record doesn't always represent the best candidate for promotion into sales management. Many others factors enter into it. Is the person a leader, as well as a doer? What about maturity, judgement, stability, rapport with associates and top management, and suitability for a particular area? The considerations are many. So how can you set promotional goals for yourself arbitrarily, when you really don't have complete control over them? You don't need the stress you are producing for yourself when you don't have full control of the outcome. The most rewarding formula for pursuing your goals is based on common sense, (which many times is not too common). If getting promoted into sales management is one of your goals in life, you'll be doing your utmost to realize it when you follow these rules:

> *Work hard.* Lazy people rarely get promoted. The few that do never last very long.
>
> *Keep sales up.* You can't attract management's attention with a poor sales record.
>
> *Maintain visibility.* Write memos as well as sales reports to your supervisor, supplying copies to appropriate personnel in the home office. Write about trends, competitive products, or unusual circumstances. You will become well-

known by name throughout the company. Others won't. Visibility helps considerably.

Be patient. Concentrate on making an effort, improving your sales record, and maintaining visibility regardless of how long it takes to win the promotion you feel you deserve. To become impatient causes stress. And stress, in turn, affects your performance. In addition, an impatient request for promotion may very well work against you.

Naturally, there are many other types of stress associated specifically with selling. Some are related to certain industries or unusual product lines. But *all* types are directly related to the six common sources of stress outlined in the early stages of this chapter.

TAKING CORRECTIVE ACTION

At this juncture, having thoroughly covered the various aspects of stress, let's concentrate on the corrective actions you can take to ensure your survival. To handle your stress more effectively, start practicing the following measures:

Avoid situations you know to be unnecessarily stressful and unrewarding. If you see a particular customer who's always cranky on Mondays and never fails to give you a hard time, start seeing this customer on another day. Or if you know that there's always a long line at the movies on Saturday night, choose another night instead.

Respond immediately to unavoidable situations. If customers haggle over the price every single time they give you an order and your price is firm, tell them that the price is not negotiable, why your product is worth every penny, and that there's no need to ever haggle again. And if your neighbors are constantly noisy, let them know about it. Why suffer through it night after night? They may not be aware of how noisy they are. Do your kids play the stereo too loud? Buy them earphones without delay.

"Let go" with relaxation. If you regularly "sit on" your problems, get rid of this stressful habit. Do something about a problem* so that you can then dismiss it from your mind. If stressful situations are making you tense (to any degree), do some diaphragmatic breathing (see Chapter 3). And if you need time alone for relaxation and composure, find it. Explain the purpose to those with whom you live, if they ask.

Take Inventory

Apparently the subject of stress cannot be dismissed too lightly. It is safe to say that stress is here to stay. In fact, as we continue to live longer, more complicated lives at a constantly accelerating pace, the amount of stress to which we are subjected will increase proportionately. The real question is: Are you capable of surviving the many stressful situations that await you?

Start preparing yourself to handle stress by taking an inventory of your weaknesses and strengths. Ask yourself the following questions:

- Do I fully understand stress of all types?
- Can I quickly recognize a stressful situation?
- Do I know how to cope with stress?
- Am I regularly causing stress for myself?
- Do I concentrate on avoiding stress?
- Am I willing to alter my stress-producing behavior patterns?

Be honest with yourself. You are actually dealing with how long you're going to be around on this planet. Don't bend the

*Resorting to alcohol, smoking, or drugs for the purpose of relieving tension and reducing stress is foolhardy. No help is derived relative to the solution of problems. Nothing but a masking effect is achieved, while your strength is reduced by side effects.

truth. Longevity depends on health. And while you cannot arrest the aging process, you can avoid a varied number of ailments caused by stress.

Too many people dismiss the problem of stress by claiming that they let nothing bother them. How ridiculous. I wonder what such stress-immune people would do if a tear gas bomb came crashing through the window? Then there are others who claim the ability to avoid stress completely by "doing their own thing." Are you able to do your own thing? Of course not. We are all dictated to by the very responsibilities that we choose to assume, of which there are always many. Familial, professional, and societal responsibilities form the base. And then it seems that we have responsibilities to all sorts of other people, in addition to our own commitments.

Let's face it. Where there are people there is stress. Some, however, can cope with it better than others. Those who cope well survive. They live longer and enjoy life more. If you are not already in this better-off group, start tooling up today. Most of the tools you will need are in this chapter, which is available to you as often as your motivation leads you to it.

STRESS CHECKLIST

	Always	Some-times	Never
I am able to recognize and categorize stress.	☐	☐	☐
I avoid known stressful situations.	☐	☐	☐
Imagined, unpleasant situations will cause stress for me.	☐	☐	☐
I prefer to imagine the worst in the hope of eventually being pleasantly surprised.	☐	☐	☐
Loss of a sale for me is cause for much disappointment.	☐	☐	☐
I am very annoyed by prospects who won't see me.	☐	☐	☐
It is easy for me to place myself in the other person's shoes.	☐	☐	☐
I set goals for myself that are exciting but unrealistic.	☐	☐	☐
I am able to "let go" with relaxation.	☐	☐	☐
It is easy for me to relax with a cigarette or a drink.	☐	☐	☐

Note: See Appendix section for correct answers.

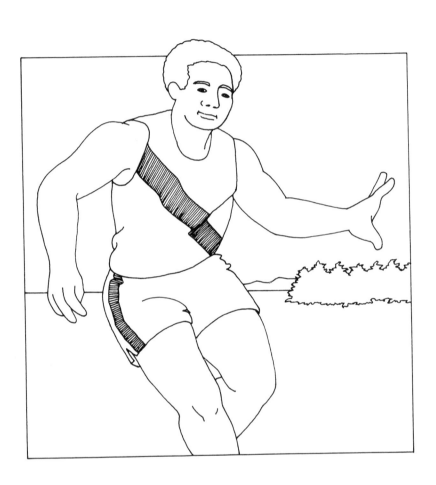

ten

FITNESS FOR A BETTER PERFORMANCE

In the business community, wellness has become a most important subject. When you look at the total picture of a business endeavor, continuous good health of the people involved in it has much to do with its success and with its ability to attain goals on schedule. Companies are becoming increasingly involved in the promotion of the good health of their employees. However, your company can only do so much for you in protecting your health. Beyond that it is entirely up to you. And no one in the company you work for is with you on a constant, daily basis to make sure that you're doing the right things for your health. Therefore, in this chapter we will be zeroing in on the many important aspects of your health that relate to your selling job. Obviously, an entire book could be written on this subject. It is vast, to say the least. Here we'll be taking the common sense approach, without getting too technical, to cover the do's and don'ts that apply to your general daily routines.

SELLING TECHNIQUES VS. HEALTH

Most of us spend much time and effort to become better at the selling process (reading this book is a good example). This usually involves refining the various selling techniques and sales strategies that help us to get the order when we need to get it. But it doesn't take an intellectual genius to figure out that no matter how good we become at the selling process, our expertise is useless if we're not able to go out and make the sales calls. You have to stay well in order to make sales calls. You must feel well to make them enthusiastically and effectively. The next question is: how well is 'well'? If you're sufficiently nourished, if you're able to make sales calls, and if you're able to get a decent night's sleep, what else is there to this business of wellness? There is a lot more.

First of all, you may feel well right now, but you may also be doing little things on a daily basis that are going to cost you down the road. And while you may feel well at the moment, you have no way of realizing how much better you could feel, especially if you never have felt that much better.

One of the big fallacies among salespeople is the deduction that since selling requires the active coverage of a territory, they get all the exercise they need to ensure good health. Well, how much exercise does a salesperson really get? If you scrutinize your daily routine carefully, you will discover that the majority of your time is spent in a seated position in your automobile, sitting in a waiting room, making a presentation while seated, sitting in a restaurant, standing in an elevator, or standing while making a presentation to a group of buyers. By comparison, the walking you do between prospects and customers will appear almost inconsequential. So how much decent exercise do you really get? Far from enough.

Fortunately, more people are becoming aware of this fact and are actively pursuing longer, healthier lives through physical fitness. They have decided that in our highly mechanized and sophisticated society we must learn to use and care for that most complex and productive of all machines—the body.

Are you ready to join the increasing ranks of physically fit salespeople?

HOW TO KEEP PHYSICALLY FIT

First of all, it will serve a good purpose to define physical fitness. About the best definition I've seen comes from a booklet entitled, *Physical Fitness, We Support It* published by North American Rockwell Phillipps Petroleum Company. The definition is as follows:

Physical fitness is the ability to carry out daily tasks with vigor and alertness, without undue fatigue, and with ample energy to enjoy leisure time pursuits and to meet unforseen emergencies. It is the ability to last, to bear up, to withstand stress, and to persevere under difficult circumstances where an unfit person would quit. Physical fitness is more than "not being sick" or merely "being well." It is different than immunity to disease. It is a positive quality, extending on a scale from death to abundant life. All living individuals, thus, have some degree of physical fitness, ranging from the severely ill to the highly trained athlete. It varies considerably in different people and in the same person from time to time, but affects one's activities to some degree *all the time*.

Naturally, you will want your sales activities to be affected by physical fitness in a positive rather than a negative way. Now let's go over some of the things you should be doing.

Exercise Regularly

At the top of the list, of course, is exercise. Frankly, however, some of the books available on exercise and body building go to extremes. You don't need to develop a fantastic muscular physique in order to succeed in selling. That should be left to the athletes and the body building buffs. All you need do is develop a program of regular exercise. If done sporadically it doesn't do much good. Done regularly, exercise will change your entire state of wellness.

Many leisure activities involve substantial exercise: swimming, tennis, handball, racquetball, softball, golf, and others. But most people engage in such activities only on weekends. Unless you have your own swimming pool and make a point of taking a vigorous swim each day, you cannot count on these activities to provide the exercise you need. You must develop a plan of some kind whereby you are able to exercise everyday. You may want to do it upon arising in the morning, in the form of calisthenics, or in the evening (well after dinner). If you have a small enough territory, you may stop in at a health spa during your lunch hour and take your exercise in that way. Whatever the plan, the secret is to do it on a daily basis.

Many people turn to jogging. Now, this is a fine form of exercise. But so much has been written on the subject that it requires qualification at this point. When jogging became the "in thing" to do, it was amazing to see how many people took to the roads in the early morning or late evening, in a display of tremendous will power. But after a while the authorities decided that jogging was not good enough. You had to run to make it all worthwhile. Then everyone began running instead of jogging, and puffing like they never had before. Not long after that, a few books were written stating that running is not the answer either. These books warn that unless the heart is in top condition, you can do a lot of damage with running. Brisk walking, they say, is better for the average American who wants to exercise for health purposes. Well, I was one of the joggers who became completely confused. So I compromised. I walk for 100 brisk steps and then, for the next 100 steps, I run. In order to do this alternately you have to keep track of the steps. So you end up counting, and this gives you something to do in the way of keeping your mind occupied. The end result is that you increase your respiration and heartbeat while stimulating just about every muscle in your body. But whether you choose jogging, running, walking, or a combination of your own design, I suggest that you get a medical opinion first.

Your doctor will be able to help you devise the regimen that's right for you.

All people who sell have to contend with an itinerary. After all, you must know where you're going to go and what you're going to do when you get there. It's a plan of action. Well, why not treat exercising in the same way? Have a plan. You might include it in the copy of your itinerary that stays with you. Then you can check off the exercise you do each day with the knowledge that you've just done something for your health.

Control Your Diet

Diet is the next aspect of wellness. They say that we are what we eat. Nothing could be more true, because if we eat properly we maintain good health. Most people suppose that the word *diet* means that you have to lose weight. That is true only when there is a problem of obesity. Even people who are at their correct weight, however, should still pay attention to diet—not only to maintain their proper weight, but also to avoid doing damage to the body that accumulates as the years go by.

There are many damaging things that people eat. Let's take sugar, for instance. It has been proven without question that sugar is harmful to the system, causing such problems as cavities, hypoglycemia, diabetes, heart disease, and even cancer. Yet statistics show that each American consumes more than 130 pounds of sugar per year. Now, when you consider the large number of people who avoid sugar completely, along with all those foods already containing sugar that most of us eat, the average for most people would be even higher.

You owe it to yourself to avoid sugar at all costs. If you are now using white granulated sugar in your coffee or in any other type of food, bring that practice to a screeching halt. But don't stop there. Become a label reader. Look carefully at every single label on all food items that you are going to consume. You'll be amazed at how many of them contain sugar. The ingredients listed on a label are usually ordered according to the amount of each item contained. When you see sugar listed as the second or third ingredient, you can be sure that the amount is substantial. Why eat a substance that contains only calories and no nutritional value? Accommodating your sweet tooth just isn't worth it.

Salt is another major offender. It contributes greatly to high blood pressure, heart problems, hypertension, obesity, and edema, just for starters. Many people add salt to their food even before they taste it. This not only affects health but also deadens the taste buds, not to mention the insult that it represents to the cook. Here again, you must get into the habit of reading labels. An excellent way of avoiding a great deal of salt is to buy foods that are fresh and raw. After cooking, if you are the type that likes highly seasoned food, try pepper. Chances are you won't use anywhere near as much as you would salt, and more importantly, you won't do so much harm to your body.

Certainly we should talk about meat. Most salespeople are meat eaters, particularly at dinner. However, animal fat is known to contribute to a number of health problems. Since red meat contains a great deal of animal fat, you should eat it only on rare occasions. Stick to chicken, veal and fish. Even these should always be baked or broiled, never fried. Deep-fried foods should be avoided at all cost, particularly at restaurants where the grease is used over and over again.

Salespeople are apt to grab a quick lunch, when eating alone, usually at a fast food restaurant. Nothing could be worse for your system. First of all, fast food dishes are loaded with calories, particularly the deep-fried items and those fried on top of a greasy grill. I shudder every time I hear a salesperson say, "I'll just grab a quick hamburger." In my early days of selling I used to do just that. Many times I would wonder why the hamburger would repeat on me for most of the afternoon. And in one instance they must have ground in some bad pork, because I came down with trichinosis, a disease that can prove fatal and for which there is no treatment. I was fortunate. But I learned a hard lesson.

Before I leave the topic of food, I want to make a strong plea for common sense nutrition. It seems that every time you turn around there is a new diet by a new authority being made available to the public. You've probably heard of some of them or even tried a few—the Scarsdale diet, high protein diets, high fiber diets, vegetarian diets, and low carbohydrate diets. Some of these guarantee quick weight loss while others promise maximum health benefits and increased energy. It seems, however, that the lost regimen of good nutrition derived from well-balanced, sensible meals is the real secret to a long-lasting health program. The idea is to give your body the variety of foods necessary to supply it with needed proteins, fats, carbohydrates, vitamins, and minerals. Meals should include foods, in moderation, from all of the basic food groups—milk or milk products; meat, poultry, or fish; vegetables and fruits; and cereals and breads. If you are overweight, by all means do something about it. Bear in mind, however, that crash diets are not only harmful, but that the results are only temporary as well. Any physician will tell you that losing weight slowly, on a regular program, is much healthier and enables you to keep the weight down once it's lost, even if you splurge once in awhile and give yourself a treat.

Cultivate Healthful Habits

Next we must discuss habits associated with wellness. To begin with, how are your sleep habits? Are you able to get a good night's sleep, every night? If not, you had best determine why and correct the situation. No one, in selling or not, can expect to do a good day's work without proper rest the previous night. If you have a problem with insomnia and don't know the reason, waste no time in seeing a physician.

A great many people complain that they have trouble going to sleep at night. With salespeople this is quite understandable. They have had a very active day involving considerable psychological infighting, and there are always those leftover thoughts as to why a particular sale was lost. I fell into that group very early in my selling career. Strangely enough, I began to wake up feeling tired in the morning. Then one day I discussed the situation with a physician friend. I got a fifteen-minute lecture on the importance of "turning things off" at bedtime. He pointed out to me that if I had enough will power to sell successfully, then I should use the same will power at bedtime to clear the mind of everything. At first I thought that this would be very difficult, but it wasn't. You simply place your head on the pillow and say to yourself, a few times if necessary, "I must stop thinking about everything because if I don't get a decent night's sleep I will not be effective tomorrow." If talking to yourself doesn't work for you, then think about something that makes you feel calm. Imagining yourself relaxing in a boat on a tranquil lake might be the answer, or any other mental picture that causes the proper effect for you. The end result must be a complete emptying of all thoughts. Try it. It works. You will be able to get to sleep nightly in a matter of minutes.

What other habits should you look into? Obviously, if you smoke, you know that you are shortening your life with every puff. But knowing that is one thing and doing something about it another. Admittedly it takes a great deal of will power, but you can do it if you really want to. Look at it this way: you are not only causing substantial injury to your own health, but you are also affecting the health of others around you—your family, friends, customers, and anyone else who is forced to inhale your smoke. Does that make you feel guilty? I hope so. Life is short enough as it is.

Naturally, we have to discuss the habit of drinking alcoholic beverages. If you don't drink at all, wonderful. If you do take an occasional social drink, make sure it's occasional. It is common knowledge that one or two drinks before dinner is good for your blood circulation. But you really do not need one or two drinks every single night. That is strictly habit. Here's a good attitude to adopt. You know that you want to keep your weight within normal limits. Very well, then. Look at the labels on liquor bottles. The Scotch that's 86 proof represents 86 calories in each ounce. The bonded bourbons are 100 proof, and that means 100 calories per ounce. If you add ginger ale or any other sweet soft drink you can add approximately 65 calories more to each drink. Tall drinks, like a Tom Collins, hover around the 350 calorie mark. Martinis and Manhattans may look like small drinks, but they are big in calories. The vermouth brings the total of each to 150 calories. And this doesn't include the olives or the cherries. "Ah, well," you might say, "I'm glad I stick to beer." In case you didn't know, beer has 200 calories in a bottle and ale 300. Should you have a taste for bock beer, each bottle has 370 calories. That's as many calories as you would find in a chocolate ice cream soda. How about improving your circulation while relaxing completely through dinner by sipping on a glass of dry wine. It will only have cost you 75 calories.

Get an Annual Physical

I'm sure that you're very conscientious about your salesmanship. Proof of that is that you've gotten this far in this book. But are you as conscientious about checking the curve of your health as you are about checking your sales curve periodically? The annual physical is a must for everyone, particularly for people who have reached the age of thirty-five. There are many medical problems that develop only gradually. Symptoms do not come to the surface, on many occasions, until a problem is completely out of control. There are many people, for example, who have high blood pressure, diabetes, or both and don't know it. They don't go for annual physicals and thereby keep themselves in the dark. Many lives are lost that way, unnecessarily.

To ensure wellness, get in the habit of having an annual physical. Ask your doctor to send you a reminder every year, so that the period between examinations doesn't extend beyond twelve months. Too many people in selling check their automobiles more often than they check their own bodies.

Avoid Contagious Diseases

In covering your territory you come in contact with a great many people. What's more, you shake hands with most of them—something you must do. That's part of selling. But you never know what kinds of germs you may be picking up with a handshake. So it's wise to do two things. First, keep your hands out of your mouth, and wash them at every opportunity throughout the day. Second, stay a substantial distance away from people with severe coughs. And by all means, always make sure that you're drinking out of a clean glass or cup. This is especially important at restaurants in which the help may be careless.

Speaking of restaurants, more and more of them are placing bowls of mints close to the exits for customers to help themselves. This is a great practice for the image of the restaurant, but a dangerous one for its customers. With so many hands digging into the bowl during the course of a day it is possible for you to become exposed to infectious hepatitis, a disease that could knock you out of commission for two to six months. Should there be a spoon in the bowl, you will note that many people use it to transfer mints from the bowl to the hand. Consequently, the spoon comes in contact with the hand, producing the same end result. Why live so dangerously? Don't take mints just because they are free. Learn to do without them. Besides, you don't need the calories anyway.

Keep a Positive Outlook on Life

Elsewhere in this book we talked about the importance of maintaining a positive mental attitude. We said that it has a great deal to do with success in selling. Well, it also has a great deal to do with wellness. When you are a positive thinker, you always feel better. The slightest headache doesn't get you down. But it's your general outlook on life, which should always be bright, that has the most to do with your physical well-being. You'll find that most hypochondriacs are perfect examples of negative thinkers. With them, everything is going to go wrong, in addition to their health.

Give some serious thought to everything we've discussed in this chapter. Try to make constructive mental and physical habits a permanent part of your life. Chances are there are a few items that need your very personal attention, and right away. Don't be a procrastinator. Just remember that you are dealing with your health, something that becomes more precious with the passage of each year.

WELLNESS CHECKLIST

	Always	Some-times	Never
I rely on territorial coverage for needed exercise.	☐	☐	☐
I follow a plan of daily exercise.	☐	☐	☐
I avoid sugar and foods containing it.	☐	☐	☐
To flavor my food I use salt.	☐	☐	☐
For lunch or dinner I am apt to have red meat regularly.	☐	☐	☐
In place of fried foods I substitute those that are either baked or broiled.	☐	☐	☐
My eating habits consist of a well-balanced diet.	☐	☐	☐
I am able to get a good night's sleep.	☐	☐	☐
One or two alcoholic drinks, on social occasions, is the extent of my drinking.	☐	☐	☐
I follow the basic rules of avoiding contagious diseases.	☐	☐	☐

Note: See Appendix section for correct answers.

epilogue

There was a time, particularly during the 1960s, when college graduates looked down on business per se. Many considered a sales career one of the lowest forms of existence. Their goals, they felt, were set on much bigger and better things. "You can always be a salesperson," so many of them said.

Fortunately, this attitude has now been reversed, almost entirely. The many who eventually turned to a selling career discovered, the hard way, that selling is a profession; that it requires a lot more than the "gift of gab;" that it is as complicated, as deep and as demanding as any other income-producing career, if not more so; and that not just anyone "can always be a salesperson" and succeed at it.

Over ten million Americans are now involved in selling. All have found that it is a rewarding field, but only when proper effort is put into it. An increasing number have found the competitiveness so keen that survival is far from automatic. That's why this survival handbook was attempted. I say *attempted*, because to claim that *all* elements of survival in

181

selling have been included in this book would be foolhardy. The variables are so many and the psychological nuances so complex that, most likely, no one will ever document them in their entirety. I am confident, however, that I have reported herein the most important elements that I have encountered in over thirty years of selling. Salespeople, both new and experienced, will profit from at least some of them.

By having read this book you have demonstrated a genuine desire to survive and to excel in selling. You are truly commended for this. But one last word of warning: you will need to reread these pages several more times, for now, and then periodically throughout your selling career. Why so many times? Because the human mind is like a sieve. As fast as you put things in, they slip right out again. All you can do is to continue putting things in—over and over again—in the hope that some will stick to the sides.

Keep smiling.

appendix

ATTITUDE CHECKLIST

	Always	Some-times	Never
I have good control of my ego.	X		
I have a strong desire to do a better selling job.	X		
I have a good attitude toward myself.	X		
I tend to place buyers on a pedestal.			X
I have a good, balanced attitude toward my prospects and customers.	X		
I will fight hard with company officials to satisfy a customer.			X
When deserved, I make critical remarks about my company.			X
I find myself doing a certain amount of negative thinking.			X
I worry about problems, personal and otherwise.			X
In an anxious situation I expect the worst.			X

I set high goals for my-
self.   ☐ X   ☐   ☐

I am able to maintain a
positive mental attitude.   ☐ X   ☐   ☐

Note: Any item that is checked "sometimes" requires corrective
action.

PERSONALITY CHECKLIST

	Always	Some-times	Never
I come across as an extrovert.	X	☐	☐
I give some thought to my personality.	X	☐	☐
Lost sales have been due to my personality.	☐	☐	X
I tend to boast about myself.	☐	☐	X
I look for the good in everyone and comment on it.	X	☐	☐
Volunteering opinions is something I'm apt to do.	☐	☐	X
While selling, I maintain a friendly smile.	X	☐	☐
To get an order I may tell a white lie.	☐	☐	X
I expect and get things from myself.	X	☐	☐
I make it a point to relive each sales call.	X	☐	☐
On the way to a sales call, I rehearse it in my mind.	X	☐	☐

Getting started on a Monday morning is difficult.	[ ]	[ ]	[X]
I look forward to each sales call.	[X]	[ ]	[ ]
Generating enthusiasm is easy for me.	[X]	[ ]	[ ]
Exercising patience is something I can do.	[X]	[ ]	[ ]
I am able to control my temper.	[X]	[ ]	[ ]

Note: Any item that is checked "sometimes" requires corrective action.

COMMUNICATION CHECKLIST

	Always	Some- times	Never
I speak loudly enough to make certain that people hear what I'm saying.	X		
I tend to speak louder when communicating with an older person whose hearing may be poor.	X		
I make a special effort to speak clearly by not running my words to-gether.	X		
I am aware of and try to improve upon my enunciation.	X		
I form mental images of the exact spelling of words to insure good enunciation.	X		
I avoid exaggerated enunciation bordering on the staccato.	X		
I read aloud for practice in enunciation.	X		

I practice and use dia-phragmatic breathing.	[X]	[ ]	[ ]
In selling, as well as in social conversation, I avoid uncommon words.	[X]	[ ]	[ ]
My presentation produc-es impact because I paint word-pictures with descriptive adjec-tives.	[X]	[ ]	[ ]
I am aware of my bad speech habit(s) and work at breaking it (them).	[X]	[ ]	[ ]
I sometimes record my phone conversations and play them back to de-tect poor speech habits.	[X]	[ ]	[ ]

Note: Any item that is checked "sometimes" requires corrective action.

CREATIVITY CHECKLIST

	Always	Some-times	Never
I find myself acting as a leader.	X	☐	☐
I revise my sales presentation to make it better.	X	☐	☐
I build a sales presentation around the prospect's "Hot Button."	X	☐	☐
Whenever I revise my presentation I write it out.	X	☐	☐
My sales presentation is based on the five w's.	X	☐	☐
I look for ways to think creatively.	X	☐	☐
When something is obvious I accept it.	☐	☐	X
I analyze commercials on TV and radio as an exercise in creativity.	X	☐	☐
Creative games intrigue me.	X	☐	☐
I attempt creative tasks.	X	☐	☐

Note: Any item that is checked "sometimes" requires corrective action.

SELLING TECHNIQUES CHECKLIST

	Always	Some-times	Never
I begin a sales call with a planned approach.	X		
Curiosity-arousing approaches seem to work for me.	X		
Gimmicky, attention-getting techniques bother me.			X
When using an approach based on prospect interest, I give the buyer a quick glimpse of the end result.	X		
My approaches based on appreciation may contain flattery.			X
I shake hands during the approach.	X		
Upon meeting people I'm apt to say, "How are you?"			X
I translate features into benefits for prospects.	X		
During a presentation I ask questions that produce a yes.	X		

I assume that I will get an order at each sales call.	X	☐	☐
Throughout my presentation I avoid the use of negative words and qualifying statements.	X	☐	☐
I ask for the order at least three times.	X	☐	☐
I minimize the price and magnify the returns.	X	☐	☐
In my presentation I use the word *investment* instead of the word *cost*.	X	☐	☐

Note: Any item that is checked "sometimes" requires corrective action.

OBJECTIONS CHECKLIST

	Always	Some- times	Never
Disparaging remarks against my product disturb me.	☐	☐	X
I postpone the answering of objections until the end of the presentation.	☐	☐	X
When an objection is voiced, I ask if it is the prospect's only objection.	X	☐	☐
I give prospects due respect for their viewpoints and opinions.	X	☐	☐
The answer to a frequent objection is included in my presentations.	X	☐	☐
In overcoming objections I make it a point to hit the prospect's Hot Button.	X	☐	☐
I will sympathize with a former customer's prejudice.	X	☐	☐

If a prejudice cannot be overcome on the first call, I will return in the immediate future.   [X]   [   ]   [   ]

Verbal attacks by prejudiced customers disturb me.   [   ]   [   ]   [X]

When a prejudiced customer shouts, I use the "speak softly" technique.   [X]   [   ]   [   ]

I am patient and tolerant in dealing with buyers.   [X]   [   ]   [   ]

I will accept blame, even when not deserved, to keep a buyer happy.   [X]   [   ]   [   ]

Note: Any item that is checked "sometimes" requires corrective action.

SALES STRATEGIES CHECKLIST

	Always	Some-times	Never
As soon as I have waited ten to fifteen minutes to see a prospect, I take proper action.	X	☐	☐
The "too busy" response stirs me into aggressively seeking a luncheon or "eat-in" situation.	X	☐	☐
I recognize and properly handle "freeloaders."	X	☐	☐
I control any drinking when dining with a prospect.	X	☐	☐
I avoid making a presentation over lunch until the meal is over and no further interruptions are expected.	X	☐	☐
I remove my coat before making a sales presentation.	X	☐	☐
Politely, I turn down coffee offers made by prospects.	X	☐	☐
I refrain from smoking during a presentation.	X	☐	☐

I attempt to get on a
first name basis with
prospects and custom-
ers.   ☒   ☐   ☐

I am able to properly
handle egotists.   ☒   ☐   ☐

My presentation utilizes
the Socratic style of
salesmanship.   ☒   ☐   ☐

I avoid discussing busi-
ness when socializing
with prospects or cus-
tomers.   ☒   ☐   ☐

I have trouble remem-
bering people's names.   ☐   ☐   ☒

Note: Any item that is checked "sometimes" requires corrective
action.

ASSERTIVENESS CHECKLIST

	Always	Some-times	Never
I'm able to make a presentation without being cut off.	X		
My verbal communication is positive.	X		
I speak up firmly when unfair demands are made of me.	X		
I'm able to get people to do things my way, cooperatively and without disdain.	X		
When making a presentation I sit up erectly.	X		
I exercise my assertiveness, even on little things, to stay in trim.	X		
I can exercise power over prospects without antagonizing them.	X		
I feel considerable power, gained from assertiveness, when asking for the order.	X		
I expect a prospect to say yes at the close.	X		

Certain people are able
to take advantage of
me.   ☐   ☐   X

If something is impor-
tant I stand up for it.   X   ☐   ☐

When I decide that I
made a wrong purchase
at a "final" sale, I still
try to return it.   X   ☐   ☐

Note: Any item that is checked "sometimes" requires corrective
    action.

STRESS CHECKLIST

	Always	Some-times	Never
I am able to recognize and categorize stress.	X		
I avoid known stressful situations.	X		
Imagined, unpleasant situations will cause stress for me.			X
I prefer to imagine the worst in the hope of eventually being pleasantly surprised.			X
Loss of a sale for me is cause for much disappointment.			X
I am very annoyed by prospects who won't see me.			X
It is easy for me to place myself in the other person's shoes.	X		
I set goals for myself that are exciting but unrealistic.			X
I am able to "let go" with relaxation.	X		

It is easy for me to
relax with a cigarette or
a drink.

☐　　　☐　　　☒

Note: Any item that is checked "sometimes" requires corrective
action.

WELLNESS CHECKLIST

	Always	Some-times	Never
I rely on territorial coverage for needed exercise.	☐	☐	X
I follow a plan of daily exercise.	X	☐	☐
I avoid sugar and foods containing it.	X	☐	☐
To flavor my food I use salt.	☐	☐	X
For lunch or dinner I am apt to have red meat regularly.	☐	☐	X
In place of fried foods I substitute those that are either baked or broiled.	X	☐	☐
My eating habits consist of a well-balanced diet.	X	☐	☐
I am able to get a good night's sleep.	X	☐	☐
One or two alcoholic drinks, on social occasions, is the extent of my drinking.	X	☐	☐

I follow the basic rules
of avoiding contagious
diseases. | X | [   ]   [   ]

Note: Any item that is checked "sometimes" requires corrective
        action.